VOL 2

A VIEW FROM
THE ★ TOP

*Avon's elite leaders share their stories
and strategies to succeed*

Foreword by Lisa M. Wilber

THRIVE Publishing
A Division of PowerDynamics Publishing, Inc.
San Francisco, California
www.thrivebooks.com

Although the publisher has made every effort to ensure that the information in this book was correct at press time, the publisher does not assume and hereby disclaim any liability to any party for any loss, damage, or disruption caused by errors or omissions, whether such errors or omissions result from negligence, accident, or any other cause.

ISBN: 978-0-9897129-1-0

Library of Congress Control Number: 2012950163

Printed in the United States of America on acid-free paper.

URL Disclaimer: All Internet addresses provided in this book were valid at press time. However, due to the dynamic nature of the Internet, some addresses may have changed or sites may have changed or ceased to exist since publication.

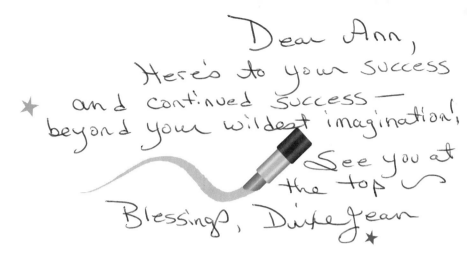

Dear Ann,
Here's to your success
and continued success —
beyond your wildest imagination!
See you at
the top
Blessings, Dixie Jean

We dedicate this book to you...

our reader; the Avon® representative, the direct seller, the entrepreneur, whether you are experienced or just getting started. You recognize the power of learning from others who have accomplished what you seek to achieve. We salute you for embracing knowledge and allowing our stories and success strategies to enhance your life and advance your career. We celebrate your commitment to being the best you can be!

**The Co-Authors of *A View From The Top Volume 2:*
Avon's elite leaders share their stories
*and strategies to succeed***

In Memory of Sophia Smith ★

A life beautifully lived, a heart deeply loved

There is no better dedication to Sophia than this book. In the true Avon spirit, Senior Executive Unit Leaders tell their success stories and share their knowledge and strategies to help you on your journey to success. These leaders work with a servant's heart and know the key to success is helping others. Sophia's passion was transforming lives, a passion the entire Avon family shares. Enjoy and save this book— within it are the secrets to building your business—perhaps you will write the next chapter. If Sophia were alive today, she would tell you that a dream is just a dream until you physically make it happen.

On behalf of Jeff, Zach, Karen and myself, I thank our Avon family for their support. I will never forget the love they showed my family and will work forever to repay it. ALS took Sophia's life, yet her spirit lives on forever in the hearts of her friends and family within Avon.

Thank you and God bless you all,
Randy Smith, Senior Executive Unit Leader

Ask me about *The Ride of Life,* my tribute ride on my Harley® to the four corners of the United States. I share Sophia's story and the impact Avon, ALS and Hospice has on lives. If 200,000 people each donate $10, we will name the upcoming in-house facility serving Hospice of South Texas *The Sophia Smith Center of Compassion.* Contact me at smithavon@yahoo.com for more details and ways you can help.

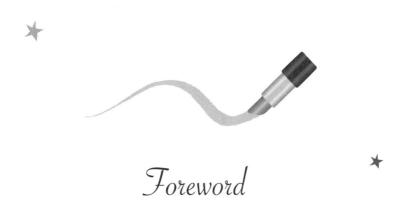

Foreword

"Somebody should get the Senior Executive Unit Leaders together and have them write a book. Think of all the inspirational stories and ideas they could share," I said to myself for *years*. *Somebody* should really do that. It was not until January 2012 that I realized *I* was that somebody! I made the call to my publisher friend Caterina Rando and she worked on the project specifications for the book. I started calling my Senior Executive Unit Leader friends and told them my idea. *A View From the Top* was born! Since that revelation, the project has expanded to include an audio interview flash drive with the authors and *Volume 2,* which you are holding in your hands. Between the two books, 47 of Avon's top producers have shared their stories of heartbreak and triumph and given solid, real-world advice on how you can achieve more, too. This project has definitely been a labor of love. Holding the books and flash drives in my hands feels like holding a dream come true. Do you have a dream that you think *somebody* should do? Why not you? Why not start today? This book and the one before it are proof positive that one person's dream, when acted upon, can change lives. Start with yours. Isn't it time you took action on your dreams?

Lisa M. Wilber, Author, Speaker, Entrepreneur
733 S. Stark Hwy., Weare, NH 03281
www.winnerinyou.com
www.facebook.com/winnerinyou

Table of Contents

Acknowledgements   xi
Introduction   xiii

Put People First and Profits Follow   1
By DixieJean Cunningham

Replace Fear with Faith and Live Your Dream   13
By Tawana Lyles

Swimming to Success   25
With Passion, Persistence and a Plan
By Anita Albaghli

From Financing to Financial Freedom   37
By Francine McDonald

It's the Journey: Onward!   47
By Molly Stone-Bibb

Painting the Canvas of Your Dreams   57
By Dan and Jackie Mundy

Transformation at Its Best   67
By Laura Douglas-Robinson

Where the Lord Leads   77
By Paula Weatherly

It Started with a Dream   87
By Claudette and Murtain Haskin

Our Climb to the Top   97
By Pete and Gerry Colbath

A Journey to Success   109
By Marie Benoit-Wilcox

Take Action to Achieve Your Dreams   119
By Angela Kokorudz

My Avon® Legacy 129
By Donna Reid-Mitchell

Your Past Does Not Make Your Future 141
If I can achieve it, so can you!
By Jo Ann Potts

Believe in Your Dreams 151
By Karen Tucker

Changing a Hobby into a Million Dollar Business 163
By Lisa Scola

Time, Dedication and Motivation Create Success 173
By Maria Street

Play Big 183
to Live Big
By Pam Knight

Achieving the American Dream 193
By Esther Lunis

Roll Around in the M.U.D.—Master Your Ultimate Desires 203
Roll up your sleeves and dig deep to find your inner hidden treasures
By Carrie Purgason

Success Is a Journey, Not a Destination 215
By Kendall Cronk and Maria Delgado-Cronk

Dreams Do Come True! 225
By Pam Heller

Make Success Attainable: Working Strategically to Grow Quickly 237
By Rosemarie Osolinsky

Dream, Believe, Achieve 247
By Chris and Gingermichele Kapp

Reach Your Potential to Make Your Dreams Come True 257
By Rosa De La O Gomez

More *A View From The Top Volume 2* 267
Geographical Listing for *A View From the Top Volume 2* 268
You're Invited... 270
Get Published With THRIVE Publishing™ 272
Other Books from THRIVE Publishing™ 274

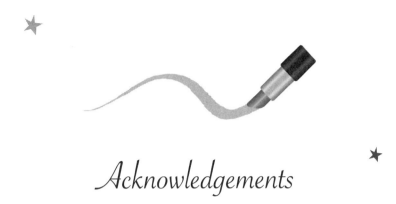

Acknowledgements

An important element for succeeding in business is gratitude. We would like to express ours here, to those who have turned our vision for this book into a reality.

This book is the brilliant concept of Lisa Wilber, who shared her story in the first volume of *A View from the Top*. She realized how valuable our collective knowledge and experiences would be to those who truly strive to succeed in their businesses. The result was putting our ideas into a second, comprehensive book to share our stories and strategies. The first book was such a success and helped so many people that Lisa put the wheels in motion for this second volume. We are grateful for Lisa's vision.

Caterina Rando is the founder of Thrive Publishing and a respected business strategist and speaker. Without Caterina's "take action" spirit, her positive attitude and her commitment to excellence, you would not be reading this book of which we are all so proud. She was supported by a dedicated team who worked diligently to put together the best possible book for you. We are truly grateful for everyone's stellar contribution.

To Karen Gargiulo, who served as project manager and copyeditor for this book, we appreciate your patient guidance and the expertise you shared to ensure that this book would be the best it could be.

To Noël Voskuil and Tammy Tribble, our designers extraordinaire, who brought their creative talents to the cover and book layout, thank you both for your enthusiasm, problem solving and attention to detail throughout this project.

To Monique Cabading and Rua Necaise, who provided us with keen proofreading eyes, thank you for your support and contribution and for making us read so perfectly on paper.

The Co-Authors of *A View From the Top Volume 2:*
Avon's elite leaders share their stories
and strategies to succeed

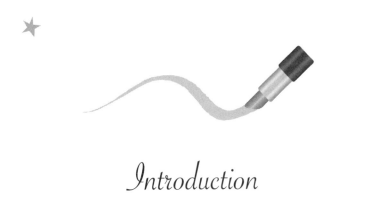

Introduction

Congratulations! You have opened an incredible resource, packed with inspiring stories from Avon's top representatives. You are about to discover our proven strategies for success. These methods can work for you, too.

In these pages, you will learn how elite leaders went from humble beginnings to building amazing, successful businesses that let them live the lives of their dreams. Some of the co-authors of this book reveal how they managed to triumph in the face of adversity. Others expose how what seemed to be the end of their working lives would only prove to be the beginning of something much bigger.

This book is loaded with tips you can use today to grow your business. It is also highly motivational, as we have each reached the highest levels of the pay scale in the Avon company. It's all here—how-to's for working your Avon business into an achievement you never thought possible.

All the Avon experts you will meet in this book want you to realize that you can dream big and accomplish your goals if you choose to. If you take action and apply the strategies, tips and tactics we share in these pages, you will reap many rewards. With our knowledge and your action, we are confident that you too will build your confidence and succeed.

Some bits of advice are repeated in different chapters—that tells you how important that advice is! We hope our stories motivate and empower you to reach for your dreams.

To you and your continued success!

The Co-Authors of *A View From The Top Volume 2:*
Avon's elite leaders share their stories
and strategies to succeed

Put People First and Profits Follow

BY DIXIEJEAN CUNNINGHAM

"Life is like a camera; focus on what's important, capture the good times, develop from the negatives and if it goes wrong... take another shot."
—Author Unknown

I was welcomed into this world by my parents, two older sisters and a medical staff amazed that I was a healthy newborn. A few days before I was born, my mother was hospitalized and diagnosed with polio. She underwent an emergency C-section while in an iron lung. I was born inside the iron lung. Polio paralyzed my beautiful mother from the neck down.

My dad was just starting in dental school when he, too, was diagnosed with polio. His case was milder and he fully recovered with only a residual of weakness in his shoulders.

My childhood memories of growing up in North Florida with my parents and two sisters were very happy, fun and carefree times. My mother was one of the most positive people I have ever known. She laughed easily, loved people and I do not remember her ever feeling sorry for herself. She learned to type with her teeth using a typing stick and wrote letters daily to people all over the world. When I was very young she sold Avon® and loved it. She often participated in fundraisers for our church. I became her helper and the seed of entrepreneurship was planted.

When I was 14, my mother died from complications of polio. The first time I ever saw my dad cry was at my mama's funeral. I will always remember his tenderness, love, sense of humor and compassion with my mama, my sisters and me. Daddy remains my hero today and will be forever.

I chose nursing as a career because I had a deep desire to help others. While in college, I married Harold Cunningham, my high school sweetheart and love of my life. I graduated six months later. As a registered nurse, I worked many years in different nursing fields, trying to find my niche in the medical field.

I also explored and joined different network marketing companies, including Tupperware®, Interior Design® and Weekenders®, yet none seemed to be the right fit.

Harold and I had been married for five years and we longed for a baby. I had a difficult time getting pregnant and my doctor prescribed fertility drugs—which worked! My prayers were answered when nine months later our first daughter was born. Two years after her, our baby daughter came into this world. My girls are precious gifts from above. I found complete fulfillment the moment I became a mother. Being a wife and mother is my greatest joy and blessing.

Fast forward to the autumn of 2004. Our daughters had grown and were living on their own. We were empty nesters. I was working long hours in the medical field, taking 24-hour on-call duty and experiencing less control over my time. I felt irritable, tired and overworked. I knew I could not go on physically, mentally or emotionally in my nursing career. Even on my days off, I dreaded going back to work. I yearned for a big change in my life.

Discovering the Right Fit

That change came in the form of the decision I made on my fiftieth birthday. After praying for guidance and doing my research, I chose to make a dramatic career change. I had read Avon success stories on the Internet and I thought to myself, *I can do that—and would love it.* I joined Avon with the intention of building a success team, earning residual income and concluding my career in nursing. I was determined to replace, and even exceed, my salary with residual income. I was going for it!

My husband was not quite as enthusiastic as I was when I told him of my informed decision to start my own Avon business. "Are you kidding, have you lost your mind?" he cried. We laugh about that now. I soon found the career niche I had been searching for in the Avon network business model. I loved helping others become successful and start their own Avon business. This did not seem like work to me. It was fun, energizing and fulfilling!

Within three years of signing up with Avon, I was able to accomplish what I had set out to do. I was ecstatic about concluding my nursing career. I felt a sense of freedom—of time and of choice. Juggling my nursing job and Avon while balancing family, home and church was sometimes difficult. However, I was persistent and determined to make it work. I remember friends and sometimes family shaking their heads when I told them my plans of leaving the medical field and pursuing Avon full-time. Their looks and negative comments only added fuel to the fire within me to continue and be successful.

Personal and Professional Growth

*"You will get all you want in life, if you help
enough other people get what they want."*
—Zig Ziglar, American author and motivational speaker

My growing business grew me, too. My focus and energies expanded to developing successful leaders on my team who would, in turn, experience the growth of their own Avon businesses. I discovered that mentoring, developing and advancing leaders is the avenue to personal and professional fulfillment—and the road to financial freedom.

I am happy to say that by making a plan and taking action to work the business, goals are being achieved and lives are being changed daily through the Avon business opportunity.

Our Avon business is a way of life now. How gratifying to have a family business that will be passed on to our children and to their children. The business has provided us with the means to pay off our mortgage early and all other debts. It is liberating to be debt free. My husband's initial doubts disappeared as our Avon business enabled him to retire early after 35 years as a teacher, minister and administrator.

Avon has provided us with wonderful perks. We have traveled out west, taken trips to Jamaica and Florida, earned cash and car bonuses, received gifts, computers and leadership education. Even more valuable are the mentors and friends we have gained through Avon. Many will be friends for life.

There is nothing I value more than my faith and family. Because of our successful Avon business, we now have the resources and freedom to provide time and care to our family members when any need arises. We do not have to ask anyone else's permission for time off to attend to important things. I often say, *I will be an Avon representative and sales leader until I take my last breath.* Family and freedom are my reasons.

Leading my own Avon business has blessed me with ample opportunity for personal and professional exploration, discovery and growth. Let me share seven discoveries about myself that are making me a better Avon leader and a better wife, mother, daughter, sister and friend.

Discoveries Along the Way

1. I have discovered that aligning my life with my values—family, fun, integrity, authenticity, compassion, community, courage, loyalty and spirituality—is a non-negotiable. If I am to maintain joy, peace, energy and productivity, then I must intentionally align the way I live life and do business with my values.

2. I have discovered that I am a relational leader. I am most successful in inspiring representatives through my relationships with them, rather than through my leadership position. I have discovered that "positional leadership" is a poor approach in a business comprised of independent Avon representatives.

3. I have discovered that being sincerely authentic and transparent trumps trying to be anyone other than who God made me to be: *DixieJean.*

4. I have discovered that I am capable of mastering technology and social media resources—and that none of these can replace a personal conversation.

5. I have discovered that through mentoring people, lives can be changed. I love the opportunity Avon provides to make a difference in people's lives. How blessed I am that through the Avon opportunity, I can ask myself, *Whose life will I make a difference in today?*

6. I have discovered that in life and business, change is inevitable. Being open to change allows me to embrace new opportunities to grow personally and professionally. Being adaptable is as valuable as my business plans and goals.

7. I have discovered that people are more important than profits. Period.

Ten Success Tips to Grow Your Business

1. Schedule inspirational, informative and fun get-togethers with your team. Whether your team is big or small, decide to plan inspirational, informative and fun meetings to promote team growth. Focus on your team's accomplishments. Reward team members for their sales, recruits and efforts. I encourage my team to share their success stories and ideas. Create an Avon family atmosphere within your own team.

I have a mantra for my meetings, my three-fold focus:
The head—knowledge and information shared
The heart—a success story or a gift from the heart
The hand—free gifts for recognition of sales and recruits

I ensure that everyone who comes has fun, is recognized and does not go home empty handed. Stay within your budget, yet commit to having information, inspiration, training and updates on current incentives for your team on a regular basis. Keep it fun and focus on the team—they will want to come back. Search the Internet, Facebook® groups, blogs and so on for great information on selling and recruiting tips to pass on to your team members. Go to the library and check out motivational business books. Have drawings at your meetings and generate excitement. Focus on recruiting success at leadership meetings. Role-play prospecting with each other...keep it fun!

2. Schedule ninety-day planning sessions with your leadership representatives and those with growing consistent sales. Herein you have an opportunity to mentor, coach and recognize your stars. This is also a great tool to identify future leadership representatives whom you can help develop, discover leadership qualities and assist as needed in growing a team of their own if they choose leadership. Always focus on *their* goals and what they want to accomplish, not *your* goals. Regularly identify leaders on your team. Follow up and let them know you believe in them. Focus on mentoring and developing your "shining stars." Teach those on your team in leadership how to analyze Avon's Downline Manager (an online tool to monitor leadership business) to optimize team growth and profits.

3. Demonstrate to all your team members that they are important. Return all phone calls promptly, within 24 hours, and respond to all email inquiries and texts. This shows respect for your team members and they know you listen to their concerns and questions. Building good relationships is key to success in your Avon business.

4. Give team members a reason to stay, yet recognize that not everyone will. My mentor use to say, "Some reps will, some won't, that's okay, go to the next." Because of the very nature of network marketing, your mantra will be and ought to be next. That is okay. That being said, if you assist and help each new representative get off to a great start, answer her questions, mentor and coach her and are available for her, she has a reason to stay. Statistics show that contact with new representatives early and often, makes a big difference in their success with Avon. If a representative becomes inactive and then decides to return and sell Avon later, guess who she will call because she has had a good experience? You! Keep that in mind.

5. If you want things to happen in a big way, it is you who must make it happen. Simply take action. Prospecting is a money-making activity and essential in your Avon business. Make up your mind that you will prospect for a certain amount of time each week. Then just do it. My manager once told me, "Everyone wants to be an Avon representative, they just don't know it yet." With that in mind, go and talk to those people who are waiting for you to *ask*. Take a team member or two with you. Follow up on *every* lead and referral you receive within 24 hours. Schedule a celebration luncheon with your team members after prospecting.

6. Promote your online e-rep website. Advertise your e-rep website on your business cards, brochure labels, Facebook, emails, *everything*—for both shopping online and signing up online. Systematically ask five customers to order from your e-rep website. Host a customer appreciation online sales event for the month. Let them know that the first five customers who place an order receive a free Avon gift from you. Ask for referrals. Once your customers develop a habit of shopping online, they generally become loyal online customers for a long time. Some of them even become an Avon representative.

7. Keep a file of everyone with whom you have ever connected. Find ways to stay in touch such as Facebook, email, birthday cards and Avon brochures with your contact information. You will get business and referrals from this list over and over for years to come.

8. Connect regularly with your team through conference calls and webinars. I use freeconferencecall.com for team conference calls. For online meetings and webinars, anymeeting.com is a user-friendly site and it is *free!* Continue ongoing communication through social media, emails, texts and phone calls as well. Facebook groups are another great way to communicate with your team, recognize, inspire and provide information.

9. Have a "servant leadership" mindset. Go the extra mile for your team and others. Stay positive and upbeat as you serve and lead.

10. Explore ways in which to serve others. When you start focusing on others, you begin to make a major difference in the world. You also grow as an individual. Partner within your community for a cause you believe in such as your local humane society, a children's home in your area, or time spent at a nursing home providing hand massages with fabulous Avon products! The residents will love you for it and it could even lead to increased sales and recruits.

Aspire to be More

> *"Your income is determined by how many you serve and how well you serve."*
> —**Bob Burg, American bestselling author and speaker**

Whatever your dreams and goals are, say them out loud, write them down, and have your mind made up that you will succeed in your business. Find your Avon niche!

Take Action:
- Stick with it and keep showing up.
- Clarify your values, goals, plans, motives and methods. Write them all down.
- Take action on your written plans.
- Remember, small steps toward your goals done consistently— daily—over time result in big accomplishments and big success.
- Keep at it. Stay positive. Keep it simple. Keep it fun.
- Maintain a healthy balance while growing your business. Take regular time off to rejuvenate.

- Read, read, read—for information, inspiration and motivation.
- Focus on service rather than sales and on people rather than profits—profits will follow!

You can be successful! Do you have the desire, determination and a can do attitude? Do you enjoy helping others? Take those qualities, and your God given skills, and decide to succeed in your business. You can have the life and legacy you wish to create for yourself and your family. Dreams do come true.

DIXIEJEAN CUNNINGHAM
Avon® Senior Executive Unit Leader

(478) 542-0757 (cell)
joinavon2day@gmail.com
www.dixiejean.net
FB page: www.dixiejean.biz
www.start.youravon.com, code: dixiejean

DixieJean worked as an R.N. for thirty years, including several years as a marketer in the health care field. During this period, she joined different companies in the direct sales industry searching for a profitable niche. Family and her children have always come first in all her career decisions.

With determination and a desire to succeed in network marketing, DixieJean made a life-changing decision to start her own Avon business in 2004. Within three years, she walked away from the security and salary of her medical career. In 2011, DixieJean achieved her dream of reaching the highest rank in Avon's multi-level network and became a Senior Executive Unit Leader. Her team received the number one Southeast area award for total unit sales increase in 2012 and reached a milestone in 2013 when annual team sales generated over 1.5 million dollars. Many have heard DixieJean express that the key to success is helping others reach their goals and dreams.

In an effort to continue making a difference, DixieJean donates a portion of her online profits to Noah's Ark for the Rehabilitation of Animals & Children.

Replace Fear with Faith and Live Your Dream

BY TAWANA LYLES

As a child, I always had a drive to succeed. I lived in the small town of Natchez, Mississippi. I grew up living with my mom, younger sister and two brothers. By the time I was 12 years old, an entrepreneur was in my blood. I learned to braid hair. I mastered the art by practicing with my own hair. People in the neighborhood started asking if I would braid their hair, which I did free for a while and then decided to charge a fee. I even had adult customers. It felt good to earn my own money.

Then I noticed a lady who had a booming neighborhood business selling freeze cups. I became one of her loyal customers. She could not keep up with the demand. It occurred to me that I could sell freeze cups along with hair braiding services. Business was booming! Surprisingly, the lady started coming to me for business.

I knew then that someday I wanted to own my own business. My last year in high school, I took an extra trade for business. I wanted to attend a four-year college after high school, however I was denied. I was devastated. I applied for jobs constantly while still living at home and no one hired me for a year.

Jobs were scarce in my small town. Adults took the few jobs that were available, even fast food positions; therefore people coming out of high school had no work. I made money picking pecans during the fall.

I was determined to make a change in my life. At age 19, I found an ad in the newspaper about becoming an Avon® representative and happily signed up. I walked the entire neighborhood, knocked on every door and sold nothing! I wanted desperately to at least make a living for myself and move in to my own place.

Then my best friend introduced me to Leon. We went out on group dates with two other couples, who were friends. I was not interested in him at the time and just went out with him because of my friends. Ultimately, however, we fell in love.

I shared my dream with Leon of taking business courses and starting my own business. He vowed to help me. He had his own car and worked part-time, yet still lived at home with his parents. Leon took me to Jackson, Mississippi, and I enrolled in Southern Technical Business College. He took me to school every day—nearly a two-hour drive!

Leon lost his local job because he was not making it to work on time. At one point, we did not have enough money for gas to go home to Natchez. We stayed in Jackson and slept in his car, determined that I would continue my schooling. We had faith.

Finally, we moved to Jackson with very little money. Not even enough for the first month's rent. We found a move-in special for 99 cents for the first month and got the apartment. Now we had to find jobs. I knew there was a higher power looking over us. Soon we found part-time jobs and invited my best friend and her boyfriend to move in with us. They also found jobs and we were able to share rent in our one-bedroom apartment.

I graduated from business college with a 3.11 grade point average. What a happy day! I soon landed a job working for a well-known law firm called Davis, Goss and Williams. They gave me my first break. Things were falling into place.

Later, I worked for the United States Bankruptcy Courts. I married my boyfriend—my knight in shining armor, Leon Lyles, Jr. We now have three children together and are buying our own home. Although our jobs paid fairly well and provided benefits, I was missing something. I still had a burning desire to own by own business.

I joined Avon again in 1993 in order to earn extra money for family activities and self-shopping sprees. Avon was quite popular with my office colleagues and close friends and I made President's Club in no time. I grew to love the products. Despite the growing sales, I still did not see Avon as a real earnings opportunity. Because I did not attend Avon meetings, I was not aware of the benefits.

Life-Altering Moment

I attended an Avon conference in Orlando, Florida, where leadership representatives shared information about the unlimited money you could earn through leadership. This was the *Aha!* moment when I realized Avon was it for me. My dream to own my own successful business was about to come true—with Avon. I had made up my mind and I was determined to succeed—failure was not an option. I had no mentor or upline and there were no local leadership representatives in my area with whom to network. I taught myself the business through trial and error.

Three Vital Steps for Success

I have boiled down the three most important steps I took to achieve my dreams with my business. I encourage you to take action on these vital steps too.

1. Read, read, read. Read everything you can get your hands on related to Avon leadership. Make sure you fully understand the earnings and qualifications on each leadership level. Watch the Avon *Rich and Famous* video—I watched it over and over and envisioned myself in the video.

2. Set goals and believe. Set a goal to succeed and believe in yourself. I set a goal to become an Avon Senior Executive Unit Leader (SEUL) from the beginning. I believed I could make it to the top.

"If someone else achieved it, then it is possible!"
—Les Brown, American businessman and motivational speaker

3. Take time for self-development. Expand your knowledge and develop your skills—become an expert. I participated in all of Avon's online trainings. I mastered youravon.com and Downline Manager. Absorb all of Avon's resources. I read stories about other successful Avon representatives in the *Spotlight* to stay motivated. Self-development is important to your success and that of your team. It is a non-stop process.

How I Built the Business

I knew in order to make it to SEUL, I had to take massive steps to grow. I had a talk with my husband to let him know my plan and asked for his support. I would need to spend a large amount of time building the business. I grew my downline by prospecting in malls, grocery stores and everywhere I went. Later, I invested in job fairs, career fairs, newspaper ads, flea markets and festivals. Keep in mind, I was still working a full-time job, my children were very active in sports and I remained active in church. When you want something badly enough you will not let anything stop you. You will find the time. Excuses will not be an option. Have a plan and stick to it. Consistency is the key to success.

Training, Developing and Conquering Fear

My downline was growing rapidly and it was time to start having group trainings. Meeting each recruit one-on-one was no longer working because of my limited time, but I had feared speaking in public all my life. The thought of getting up and speaking would send me into a state of shock. When I stood up to speak, my thoughts sat down. I realized that in order to succeed and help others succeed, I had to conquer this fear that was holding me back. I prayed to God to see me through it. Each time I got up to speak, I asked God to help me focus and to use me to help others with encouraging words. It became easier each time I spoke.

I discovered that the Bible has all the answers and is the guide to living a happy and peaceful life. I found we need this balance to live our dream.

I know beyond a doubt that God is with me and is blessing me. In return, I bless others by giving, sharing and spreading the good news of His goodness.

"I can do all things through Christ which strengtheneth me."
—Philippians 4:13

Transitioning from Full-time Employment

The time had come to live my dream. Honestly, I was scared to take the life-altering step of quitting my job. I had been with the U.S. Courts for 17 years and made over $56,000 per year with benefits and a retirement plan. I could have been like most people and decided to remain where I was comfortable. However, I just could not live the rest of my life wondering *What if?* Plus, I was not happy working from eight to five every day. I always wanted freedom of time, freedom of unlimited earnings and freedom to give.

Others thought I had lost my mind when I announced I was leaving my long-term job to work an Avon home-based business. Some tried to talk me out of it. My husband gave me the okay, yet I could see in his eyes he was somewhat skeptical. However, he loved me enough to support me in taking this step.

I remembered my last day at work. Emotions were all over the place. I would miss my office colleagues. Then fear set in again. *What are you going to do now? What have you done? Are you crazy?* I had to get rich or die trying. I had to win! I surely was not going to let fear take root. I prayed to God for strength and wisdom, and worked my business full force. I kept a full schedule at all times.

Avon became a family business. My sons and husband helped build the business by working flea markets and festivals on weekends.

They loved the selling part, which taught my sons to earn their own money. Having family time while working our business brought us closer together.

Striving for Success Through the Ups and Downs

Business and life have their ups and downs. I lost my SEUL title twice. The first time was shortly after I left my full-time job. I was devastated! Others would have taken the easy way out and given up by going back to work. However, I would not give up! My dream was still alive. I am a fighter. I got back up and worked another plan—and worked harder.

> *"When obstacles arise, you change your direction to reach your goal, you do not change your decision to get there."*
> **—Zig Ziglar, American author and motivational speaker**
> **Living the Dream**

I can now say I am living my dream. At this point I just cannot imagine working for someone other than myself. I am an SEUL with an over $2 million growing business. I have the freedom to give and share with others and to spend more time with my family.

I have time to build my team and teach them everything I know. You get a great feeling when you have shared something that can genuinely help someone. Our group trainings draw my team and me close like family. I care for them and their well being more than they will ever know. Therefore, I create well-planned trainings, not simply social gatherings. I make sure they gain something from it.

My goals are ongoing and one of them is to share the business and change as many lives as I can. Another ongoing goal is to motivate and help others to have faith and keep dreaming. I plan to build ten SEUL's within the next one to two years.

Unfortunately, many people do not see Avon as a real earnings opportunity. My team and I plan to show the world that is not the case. I challenge all Avon representatives worldwide and those interested in the Avon opportunity to join me on this crusade.

Words of Wisdom

Keep growing. There are plenty of resources you can tap to become an expert.

- Take advantage of Avon online trainings.
- Master the website, youravon.com.
- Read motivational and network marketing books.
- Participate in Avon conference calls weekly or playback recordings.
- Partner with other successful Avon representatives and friend them on Facebook®.
- Know your products.
- If you are a leadership representative, use Downline Manager daily to track your team.
- Encourage team members to develop themselves. Teach and show them how. If they are not willing, put your energy into those who are. Some will be fast learners and some will not. Have patience with them and invest your time in them if they are willing to learn and work. Strive to be a true leader.

Have a plan and weekly schedule. You never wake up and wonder, *What am I going to do with my business today?* Always have your schedule prepared. I see a lot of businesses fail or stay stagnant because they fail to have a plan or weekly schedule. Have a to-do list in writing. Be consistent with your schedule and you will succeed.

Be a master appointment maker.

- Take your time to get to know your prospects during appointments.
- Interview them so that you know how to help.
- Discover the emotional reason why they came to Avon.
- Create excitement!
- Help them believe in themselves and in the business.
- Let them know you are there every step of the way to help them succeed.
- Help them with the Invitation List, formerly known as the *Who Do You Know?* list.
- Show them the money through the Believe in Your Success leadership program.
- Follow up within 48 Hours to reconnect to their *why* and discuss the Invitation List.

Be yourself.

- Do not compare yourself to others.
- Give it your all and work hard to improve yourself. In time, you will be comfortable at what you do and you will soar.
- Learn from others and be happy for people who are successful.
- Run your own race and be the best you!

Have a positive mind set at all times.

- Surround yourself with positive people.
- Speak positively around others.
- Do not engage in negative conversations.
- Lift others.
- Do not complain about the small things—a habit that could kill your spirit and your strength. Also, you could unknowingly pass this bad habit on to others. We need our strength to endure.

Teach your team to schedule event activities weekly or monthly.
- Set up a table at job fairs, career fairs, local businesses, community events, festivals and yard sales.
- Make sure your table is professional and dress professionally.
- Be well prepared.
- Strive to impress—they are watching.

Always Follow Up.

Are you ready to live your life? Then put away the fear of the unknown that has been hindering you from living a fulfilling life. Find your God-given gift. Know your purpose; step out on faith, and work. Believe in yourself and live your dream. Use the Bible as your guide to live. Do not procrastinate, as the time is now to live a financially free and fulfilled life. Use some of the business strategies from the authors of this book to move you forward. I hope we inspired you to step out on faith.

TAWANA LYLES

Avon® Senior Executive Unit Leader
Avon Success Team

(601) 259-2157
tawanalyles@aol.com
www.youravon.com/tlyles
www.start.youravon.com Code: tlyles

When she was 12 years old, Tawana thought she would someday own a successful business. She always allowed herself to dream big. Tawana started her Avon business in 1993 to earn extra money for activities with family or self-shopping sprees. She worked for The U.S. Bankruptcy Court, a well-paying job with excellent benefits. However, something was missing.

Tawana took a stand to live her dream by leaving her 17-year job to run her own full-time business as an Avon independent representative. After building her business while working her full-time job, she stepped out on faith to live the dream she is now successfully living. Tawana now runs a growing $2 million Avon business with the help of her team members, The Success Team. Tawana has always had a passion for helping others, making Avon a perfect business for her. She gives back to others and enjoys financial freedom and more time with family.

Tawana believes everyone has a God given talent and a purpose. She encourages others to take the time out to find it, to live a happy and meaningful life, and to live their dreams.

Swimming to Success

With Passion, Persistence and a Plan

BY ANITA ALBAGHLI

My Avon® story actually started when I was about six years old growing up in a small village in Ohio. I wanted to learn to swim and the most beautiful lady in the small village agreed to teach me. Every day, I would get in her car and go to the pool. Her car smelled of Skin So Soft. Her shiny black hair, beautiful skin, brightly colored lips and carefully lined eyes looked nothing like the other ladies in town. Despite her best efforts I never learned to swim. While I did not really know what I wanted to do when I grew up, I knew I wanted to make a difference in other's lives, as she had made in mine.

The years were full of moves, going to college, more moves, getting married, and more moves. My first professional job was in Corporate America and it left me drained. I would board the bus at 6:00 a.m. and get home at 7:00 p.m.—just in time to do the work I brought home and take a quick shower for the next day.

A few years later, I decided to work from home as a financial analyst. That was better, until the day my only child, Walker, was born. The companies I worked for did not seem to understand that I could get the job done; just not necessarily within the same eight-to-five timeframe they worked. I never missed a deadline, however their hours were not my hours. Therefore, I closed my in-home business and continued staying home so that I could be with my son.

Opportunity at My Door

I had been a stay-at-home mom for three years. I was feeling a bit disheartened. We rarely saw anyone during the day and did not go many places because I did not drive. When my husband came home at the end of the day, I felt quite boring because I had nothing to talk about.

One day I went to the door and found an Avon® book—the book that would change my life! I thought that maybe through Avon I could meet more people and my little guy might even find some playmates. I decided to sign up as a representative.

My first order was just $23 and my customer had four wonderful children. I was thrilled and experienced a feeling of success! Six months later, I went to my first Avon meeting and came home to let my husband know that some people actually made money at this. I told him I would learn to sell much more. I made up my mind that I would not be looking for a "real job" when Walker started kindergarten. This would be my job.

In 1999, a year after I started my business, an 11-year-old girl called and asked me if I could help her start an Avon business. We signed her mother up and she was the first of our now 750-plus team. The girl did an awesome job running her business and I became a Unit Leader within five campaigns.

I thought that was all there was to it—until I went to another meeting about six months later and met a Senior Executive Unit Leader, who was earning over $120,000 a year with her team. I went home and told my husband that I had not understood. I needed to find more people right away.

In order to do that, I renewed my focus on leadership. First I created a dream board of my ideal team. I was sure to include not only those that I wanted to personally recruit, but also a visual of future teams showing a blueprint of what was needed to move forward. I used a lot of "penny stick people" to draw my future. From there I took the following steps:

• Ran very small, affordable ads looking for representatives
• Held team meetings to encourage others to try leadership
• Looked for leaders within my team
• Canvassed customers and others for recruiting leads

Our team has slowly grown since 2000 with sales growth each year.

Including Family in Business

Had I returned to Corporate America, I would not have been able to enjoy most mornings as a "stay-at-home daughter." My parents had been living right down the street from me since my father retired and I wanted to be there for them when they needed me.

I get to visit my parents for breakfast or daily visits. I bring work with me, ask for their ideas and enlist them in helping prepare Avon books. No corporate job would have ever permitted me to spend time with my elderly parents this way.

I once read in an old etiquette book at a garage sale that a lady's job was to start her family's day off cheerfully. With Avon, I have been able to spend the first part of every day seeing my son off to school, my husband off to work, and enjoying a quiet breakfast with my parents. Avon has given me the gift of time for those who matter most. I have Avon to thank for these memories.

> *"Alone we can do so little; together we can do so much."*
> **—Helen Keller, American author, political activist and lecturer**

My family has played a vital role in my successful Avon business. My son helped me prepare for meetings and fill orders, my parents stayed active by giving me rides and bagging my books, and my husband helped me deliver orders and set up shows. There are always things we can do together!

You, too, can enlist the help of your family. Sometimes they do not realize how much the little things really count; yet their assistance with small tasks can save you valuable time. There are many ways they can help you in your business:

• Prepare for team meetings with representatives
• Fill customer orders
• Bag Avon order books
• Deliver orders to customers
• Set up products for shows

With Avon, I have earned trips to Hawaii, the Bahamas, Alaska, San Diego, and more. Mostly, Avon has given me freedom to work my own schedule, to travel, to care for my family—all while earning a six-figure income and all the niceties the earnings allow.

Self-Development with Avon

In addition to making it possible to live a wonderful lifestyle, I have truly grown as a person. Whenever I speak about the Avon opportunity, I simply blossom. Once a very shy, intensely quiet soul, I used to toss my books onto people's porches and run. I avoided long conversations with customers. However, as my business grew, so did I.

I have enjoyed speaking for Scouts, at District and Division events, and co-hosted *4 Seniors One Night* with our local Senior Executives to give representatives an opportunity to glimpse into the lives of local top leadership. I was even asked to emcee a local scholarship pageant, to my delight!

"Speech is the voice of the heart."
—Anna Marie Quindlen, American author, journalist and opinion columnist

There was a time when I lost my voice every time I spoke. Now I host many training events each year and teach sales, leadership, money management and more. I simply love coordinating events, particularly recognition events. Teaching and recognizing others is my passion! I love giving back to my team with small gifts, playing the perfect song to honor someone, and surprising unsuspecting team members with awards.

Avon has uncovered a creative side of me I never knew existed. I continue to look for new ways to have fun with my team and to motivate others. I love learning from and working with so many different personalities. No two days are alike.

Stepping Up to the Challenge

Businesses naturally go through ups and downs, and mine has too. I found myself in a bit of a rut in 2011. Our team had been million dollar producers for six years when my mentors brought it to my attention that maybe I ought to stop "playing around with my business" and get serious. They challenged me to see how much we could grow in three years. I accepted the challenge and began to strategize how I would accomplish it.

If you want to see growth in your business, I encourage you to sit down with pen and paper and develop a plan. Mine started as a three-year plan to increase sales to over $3 million per year. Here are some helpful items to include in your plan:

• Personal sales goals
• Unit sales goals
• Team title goals
• The end result
• Avenues you can take campaign by campaign to achieve your goals in each category

The last step is the most crucial. In order to achieve your goals, it is important to break each part down into small, doable activities. Action is a must in achieving your goals; therefore include action steps in your plan.

> *"A dream is just a dream. A goal is a dream*
> *with a plan and a deadline."*
> **—Harvey Mackay, American businessman and columnist**

Keep each year's plan simple by staying focused on your goals. I aimed to increase sales to $1.5 million in the first year of my plan. Although we did not fully launch the plan until July, we decided to focus solely on sales. We wanted an opportunity to help everyone on our team earn more through increasing order size. This, in turn, increased their commission earnings.

Strategies that Work

We held $1500 workshops and President's Club workshops several times that year. I had previously held my meetings in my home area. We expanded the meetings into other areas so that anyone could attend—hitting various times of day and venues. We simply taught tip after tip on building sales. Part of the program was to show representatives how I had consistently achieved Rose Circle or above for more than a decade.

We showed others how to make all the money they wanted with sales, including fundraising. We had special workshops for those selling $100 or less to show them how small changes could increase their earnings. We reached out to everyone who would work with us. Our goal was to share ways they could earn more money with as little as a $25 to $50 sales increase individually. We ended the year at $1.7 million—which was $200,000 above goal!

The following year, we turned our focus to growing our team members. We needed to go from 500 to 800 representatives to achieve our next sales goal. We continued to hold quarterly sales trainings for new representatives coming on and our main objective was to consciously work to acquire successful recruits.

We led a recruiting project we named *The 12 Weeks of Christmas,* recruiting in the field door-to-door as a team for 12 weeks. The "12 Weeks Team" committed to traveling outside their districts and learning from each other. As a result, representatives from different teams within our team built lasting relationships.

Making Your Own Luck

"Diligence is the mother of good luck."
—Benjamin Franklin, founding father of the United States

Some people may say we got lucky with our plan the second year. That was when Avon offered an opportunity to earn representatives with no upline, called nesters. Our team pulled together and worked hard to earn as many representatives as possible. Yes, we were fortunate this incentive came along, however, as with all of Avon's opportunities, it required great work to earn the nesters.

Every day, our team worked diligently on successful representatives— those who place a $100 order on time and pay for it on time. We would send out weekly follow-ups as to where each leader stood, along with ideas on how to earn more nested representatives. We closely followed the incentive to earn the maximum permitted. It was a true team effort.

I encourage you to always pursue the incentives that Avon offers. The company provides deep rewards—you can earn the prize and sustain long-term growth and stability. Short cuts rarely work, however if you build with integrity you will be richly rewarded!

Our team also had really sharpened its recruiting skills as a result of the *12 Weeks of Christmas* and the nesting opportunity by the time the *Say Yes to Avon* promotion began in 2012. We met our goal for the second year with just over 800 representatives and $2.6 million in sales.

Continue Growing

In 2013, we began our third year of the plan. We intend to reach our goal of $3 million in unit sales in 2014. We are focused on title movement and increasing the total number of units within our team by almost double. We are starting by working with those who have indicated they are interested in advancing and calculating how many units it will take to move these titles.

We will work on showing representatives how to take advantage of Avon's incentives to put more money in their pockets. We will meet regularly for support and to honor success. As always, we make it fun! We will incorporate additional sales trainings so that our teams can reach their unit sales qualifiers and our representative's can learn how to earn higher commissions.

"Real integrity is doing the right thing, knowing that nobody's going to know whether you did it or not."
—Oprah Winfrey, American media proprietor, talk show host, actress, producer and philanthropist

Above all, we will continue to teach our team "right always wins." If you show others how to be successful and to make their dreams come true through integrity and by doing the right things, you will almost certainly be a winner!

Had I not chosen to become an Avon representative when I found that book on my doorstep, and furthermore, had I not chosen to pursue all of the opportunities that Avon has available, I would not have had the family life I have enjoyed since becoming an Avon representative. Through Avon, I was able to live my dream of being a stay-at-home mom. At the same time, I could pursue a satisfying career, contribute to my family's income, and be a role model for many. I was fortunate to never miss a school event and to be home each day when my son arrived from school, from his first year of kindergarten all the way through his high school graduation.

The most important thing to remember is that all upper level sales and leadership representatives started out at one time with a first customer and a first recruit. My personal success has come from goal setting, an unflinching focus on those goals despite obstacles, and persistence. It is never too late to develop these skills and to achieve your dreams.

I still do not swim and still do not drive. However, I do remember when I was six years old and I had a very special swimming teacher who showed me things could be different.

ANITA ALBAGHLI

Avon® Senior Executive Unit Leader
Rose Circle Member
Leader of Team Freedom
(614) 837-6883
aaa4avon@yahoo.com
sellforsuccess.net
www.youravon.com/aalbaghli

Anita started her Avon business to earn extra pocket money and to get out of the house and meet people. Never did she dream her business would generate a six-figure income and that getting out of the house would mean all-expenses-paid trips to the Bahamas and Hawaii! That is a long way for Anita who does not drive.

Today, Team Freedom holds the #1 spot in the Buckeye Division for Total Unit Sales, a title the team has held since 2004. In 2012, Team Freedom was just shy of a $1 million Sales Increase placing them at #18 in the nation for Total Unit Sales Increase. Team Freedom is a national team with teams in Maryland, Mississippi, North Carolina and Ohio.

Anita dedicates this chapter to former Avon Division Manager Cindy Basler, who showed her through example that "right always wins" and inspired her to keep going and keep growing. Anita credits her success to the amazing representatives she works with every day and to her family, whose never-ending patience and support has helped her business thrive.

From Financing to Financial Freedom

BY FRANCINE MCDONALD

I was born in Brooklyn, New York. My older sister, Mary, and I lived with our parents in an apartment building they owned. My grandparents lived downstairs and my Godparents lived upstairs. I remember my family as hardworking people always striving to give their family whatever they could. Growing up I always knew that education and motivation was a good formula for success.

Early on, I knew I'd study finance. I attended college without a second thought and four years later had my bachelor's degree. I was ready to hit Wall Street with my sights set on being a stockbroker or using my credentials in the field of finance.

I worked as a finance manager for a Ford® dealership. I met my husband, Bill, at work in 1991 and we married in July of 1992. A month after we were married I landed a position as vice president of sales at a local commercial bank selling investment products as an account executive.

I loved my job and worked for ten years in a beautiful office. I moved from branch to branch meeting customers to discuss their financial needs and open investment accounts for them.

My Turning Point

After our first son, William, was born, I continued working for several years until my second son, Paul, was born. I knew that I could no longer work at the bank, as childcare would become an issue. Bill was working as a helicopter pilot police officer for the New York Police Department (NYPD). It was difficult to work around his schedule because his shifts rotated weekly.

I had to leave the bank, however I did not know what to do while caring for our sons. I became a stay-at-home mom. I loved being home with my boys and they loved having me around.

> *"Never give up on what you really want to do. The person with big dreams is more powerful than one with all the facts."*
> **—Albert Einstein, German-born theoretical physicist**

After three years, I needed to get to work. I was torn about making a decision because I did not want to leave my sons with a babysitter. That was when my mother said, "Why don't you sell Avon®?" Truthfully, I did not jump at that suggestion. I did not think selling Avon could possibly match my income working at the bank. Besides, I believed Avon was something you do on the side to supplement your income. I was unaware of Avon's Leadership program where you build a team of representatives in addition to selling products.

I started selling Avon in September 2003 and within five months I made the prestigious President's Club. I was also awarded "Best New Performer" in my district. That is when I started thinking my mother could be on to something. She had sold Avon for over 42 years. I remember way back when we lived in Brooklyn, New York, my mother taking my sister and me along with her to make deliveries to her customers in big apartment buildings. I cannot remember a time when Avon was not a part of our lives. It is funny how this came full circle for me.

Then and Now

Avon has afforded me the lifestyle I had always strived for, coupled with the flexibility I desperately needed. I have raised my children while working from home. I bought things without the constraint of a tight budget.

If you have the desire and are willing to put your ideas and energy into physical motion, you will succeed and have the things you have always dreamed of. I remember my first Avon fundraiser at my younger son's preschool. After donating a large sum of money to the school, I was still able to buy my husband a snow blower for Christmas. Of course, it hardly snowed that winter, but the following winter, Bill was a happy camper!

Bill retired from the NYPD and became an airline pilot. He flies for Jet Blue® and loves it. The job, however, takes him away from home a lot. With the flexibility of owning my own business, I am available if my boys need to stay home from school ill, I can participate in school activities, and I can go out to lunch with friends. I make my own schedule. With Avon, you set the tone.

Do you want to make a little money or a lot? That is up to you. You do not need to wait for a year-end job evaluation to get that menial raise or worry about getting laid off because of budget cuts or mergers. You live life on your terms.

My Personal Growth

Although working at the bank gave me confidence to speak to people, Avon has truly given me the ability to speak to large groups of people with ease. I remember when our division sales manager asked me to talk about fundraising at a rally being held at the Marriott Hotel®. There must have been close to 200 people there. Needless to say, I was beyond nervous. After the morning session, I felt confident that I could speak again for the evening session. It was as if I had been public speaking for years.

I have changed in other ways as well. I get to help people every day, whether it is by assisting them in choosing the right product or by guiding them in starting their businesses.

Success did not happen for me overnight. I joined Avon's Leadership program in 2004 and thought I was making pretty good money. I was satisfied with that until I went to a seminar and learned that there was even more money to be made. I wanted to get to Senior Executive Unit Leader (SEUL), which is the highest level of leadership in the Avon Leadership program.

I began getting the word out to customers, friends, neighbors and family that I was now helping others to start their own Avon businesses. I went to meetings and read self help books like this one that inspire you to strive for what you want and believe you will achieve it. I became known as the Fundraising Queen! Not only did I achieve my sales levels and increase my earnings, I recruited people from these fundraisers.

With success comes a large degree of respect and admiration. Your friends and family see the change in you and when they see your excitement and enthusiasm they truly admire what you did to get there. When Avon saw the strides I had been making, I received calls for interviews and testimonials. In December 2012, Avon asked me to represent them on *The Today Show* for their donation to the show's Annual Toy Drive. It was a great experience and the exposure enhanced my recognition. Social media was abuzz with my appearance! This was just the beginning.

Tools for Success

Social media. Many wondered how I became an SEUL without social media like Facebook®. Plenty of leaders before me accomplished this level with no social media and I felt that I was in good company. However, the big leaders today have embraced it and it has absolutely propelled their businesses forward. We live in a world where anything is possible. I recommend using everything out there to make your life easier, your business stand out, your name become well-known, and your message heard.

Success is not based on one magical quote or idea. With trial and error and discovering what works best for you where you are in life, success can be yours.

Follow up. My biggest piece of advice has always been to follow up. I tell my representatives that they must follow up. How often do you receive a catalog in the mail, look through it and toss it aside? We all do that, even when we have seen items in the catalog we want. It finds its way to a pile of other brochures or catalogs.

However, what if a representative from the catalog calls you and says, "Good Morning. We mailed you a catalog and are following up with you to see if you would like to place an order at this time." Chances are, you are thinking, *Yep, I have even folded down the pages where the items I wanted were located.* Why did you not make that call and order? Maybe the phone rang or you needed to run an errand and by the time you knew it, the kids were coming home from school and you totally forgot about that neat gadget that would have made your life a little easier. That is why we need to make those calls. You can increase your sales by hundreds in one day by following up. I have!

Recruiting from your list. When you look for business partners, I suggest you make a list of your good customers. Someone who places consistent orders could become your ideal partner. You can get her attention by showing her what she can save on her own orders and what she can make on her customers' orders. She already loves Avon, spends a good amount each campaign and often advertises for you. She wears Avon jewelry, clothing, shoes and accessories. She uses Avon skin care, makeup and fragrance. She may be pleasantly surprised to find she already has customers just because she has been showing the Avon line in normal everyday activities. I found some of my best representatives this way.

Family is also a great starting point. My aunt, for example, who took on other direct selling in the past, immediately saw the opportunity. She liked the flexibility and the idea of being a business owner. She is an Executive Unit Leader on her way to SEUL. Working with my aunt gave me a great connection with her. We always bounce ideas off one another and marvel about how our businesses are growing.

Prospect. Do not be alarmed! You actually prospect every day without even realizing it. When you recommend a movie to someone at the grocery store, you are prospecting. How is that prospecting? You are advertising the movie and enticing her to see it just because you liked it so much. Are you getting paid for that recommendation? Do you receive commission from a restaurant for talking up the dinner special you enjoyed so much? No, of course not. However, with Avon you do get paid for recommending someone into the business.

Seek opportunities. Never let an opportunity pass you by. If someone looks very well-to-do, do not feel intimidated about discussing the Avon opportunity. You do not know what her personal situation is. She just might be looking for this kind of opportunity. Maybe she is tired of her job. Maybe she makes great money, yet would rather be home with her children. Maybe she needs a nudge out of her comfort zone and does not know where to go.

Do not judge a book by its cover. I learned this through Avon. The saying is literal. I belong to a book club where we all put our pick for the next book into a hat and read the one that gets picked. Sometimes I think, *Oh no, that book looks boring,* yet that book winds up being a favorite that I recommend to others.

Participate. Set up an Avon table near a store or in a busy park and prospect for new business partners or customers. Many Avon representatives succeed with this method. Someone may be thinking, *What can I do to earn extra money?* When you offer her the Avon opportunity, it just makes sense. It clicks.

She may be thrilled to know that Avon, "The Company for Women," is designed to fit into her budget. It is the easiest sign-up procedure and lowest cost anywhere. Explain that she can receive credit in which she owes no money until after she receives the products. I do not know any other company that does this.

Access Avon support. Take advantage of Avon's outstanding support system that sets you up for success. The company gives you all the tools you need to reach your goals and dreams. Downline Manager, for example, is software that helps you to monitor what is happening within your team and recognize your team members for jobs well done. You can also partner with your district sales manager, a wonderful resource who is there to support your business.

Communicate with your team. Always listen to their concerns and devise a plan of action to maximize their business—and in turn, your own business. As with your customers, always return representatives' calls and emails, preferably within 24 hours. Building a strong foundation will leverage your business against a downturn in the economic climate or a sudden shift in competition.

I suggest you hold team and leadership meetings at least once a month. During team meetings, you can introduce new products, discuss what is or is not working in your business, share ideas, and put a plan of action into effect. During leadership meetings, you can teach new leaders how to grow their team and therefore their business. Make it fun and social! I provide desserts and refreshments as well as raffles and door prizes. Be generous with your advice and your time. As my grandmother used to say, "What you give away is never lost."

Rich Rewards

Avon is quick to recognize the accomplishments and milestones of its representatives. My Avon business has surpassed even my own expectations. Here are some rewards I have earned:

- Earned $2,500 in a contest for sales volume—purchased a 46-inch flat screen TV right before the Giants won the Super Bowl in 2008!
- Earned a 32-inch flat screen TV the following year
- Received a bonus check for $5,000 upon reaching SEUL
- Earned a Mrs. Albee Award every year since I began selling Avon, for attaining President's Club and above (the award is a porcelain replica of Mrs. Albee, the first Avon Lady)
- Earned 14 trophies, which closely resemble Oscars, for reaching a variety of goals for my district and my division

- Awarded a trip to Orlando, Florida, with a beautiful hotel room, accommodations, and a ceremony where we were treated like royalty—after graduating as one of two representatives to reach the title of SEUL in a pilot program called AUL Academy
- Earned a trip to Hawaii
- Served as guest speaker on conference calls and at meetings for various rallies
- Served as spokesperson for Avon on *The Today Show*
- Served on speaker panel at a division rally
- Featured in the *What's New* brochure of demo products, with an advice column
- Featured in the *Representative Times* bulletin "Inspirational Corner"

I encourage anyone reading my story to give Avon a good look. Explore the business and know that you can do this. So many people just like you have improved their lives with this fantastic opportunity. You will never want to do anything else.

FRANCINE MCDONALD
Avon® Senior Executive Unit Leader
Team Unstoppable

(516) 250-3249 (cell)
pilotswife777@aol.com
www.youravon.com/fmcdonald

Francine left Corporate America in 2000 after ten years as vice president of investment sales at a commercial bank. After signing up to become an Avon representative, Francine quickly soared to the top of Avon's network marketing program called Leadership as a Senior Executive Unit Leader.

Francine has a bachelor of science degree in finance from the New York Institute of Technology. She has been seen on *The Today Show* as a spokesperson for Avon's donation to the show's Annual Toy Drive. In 2003, Francine was honored as Best New Performer for District 2282 (Challenger Division). She was the recipient of the prestigious "Spirit of Avon" Award in 2010 and has received 14 awards for sales and recruiting.

Francine's husband Bill is an airline pilot for Jet Blue®. He is a great support and is very proud of her level of dedication and commitment to her Avon business and all her accomplishments. Francine resides in Garden City, New York, where she lives with her husband and two teenage sons.

It's the Journey: Onward!

BY MOLLY STONE-BIBB

This Chapter is dedicated to Ray Penn, who saw my potential long before I did. Rest in peace, my friend.

As a child, I was always a pleaser, never wanting anyone to be upset or disappointed in me, especially the men in my life. I just wanted to make the men in my life happy—from my dad, to my brothers, to my husband. I watched my mom do the same for 16 years.

Everyone loved my mom and I wanted to be loved like that too. However, life can be cruel sometimes. When I turned 17, my mom was diagnosed with pancreatic cancer and taken from me within months. This devastated my family and changed the path of my life forever.

I became angry at everyone, especially God. How could he allow this to happen? When my Dad moved on with his life a few months later,

I realized his plans no longer included me. I was lost. I disconnected from my family and moved down a path I was not prepared to travel.

After many wrong turns in life, I married my first husband and again, for 17 years, tried to make the man in my life happy. It seemed I failed time and time again.

I was blessed with two sons, Earl and Anthony, whom I love with all my heart. I tried to be the perfect wife, mother, friend, aunt and sister, and continued to be everything to everyone.

After dealing with a lifetime of emotional and verbal abuse, something in me said no more! In 2002, I uprooted my sons and left our home in the middle of the night. My brother opened the basement of his home to us and I started over again with nothing.

I had the most important things in life—my kids. After a long, angry, drawn-out divorce, I found myself with no money, no home, two jobs, a boat load of bills, and certified letters warning me that I would lose my van for being behind in payments.

I was working full-time at one job and delivering newspapers in the middle of the night two nights a week, deprived of sleep. It is amazing what you can do when you *have to.*

One night, after putting the boys to bed, I sat on my brother's front steps crying to God as I looked up at the sky. *Please God, show me what you want me to do. Show me where you want me. Give my boys something to be proud of in their mother and I promise I will give back. I will pay it forward every day of my life. Please don't let me be a failure again.* I had no idea what God had in store for me in the near future.

*"We don't meet people by accident...they are meant
to cross our path for a reason."*
—Author unknown

Fifteen years earlier, Maryann Penn, an Avon® representative, had tossed an Avon brochure in my driveway. I was thrilled because I had grown up using Avon products. I was an instant customer for her. Little did I know that Maryann would have such a huge role in my life and future. After moving to my brother's, I had no extra money and missed browsing Avon catalogs. I called Maryann and asked her to deliver to my new address.

The Impetus for Change

I was not keeping my head above water and was drowning in debt. I could barely afford a Happy Meal™ for my boys. My oldest son was going to graduate and deserved more during this important time in his life. I was determined he would have a graduation party and go to the prom. I needed additional income and had no idea how to make that happen. How would I fit in a third job?

In April 2004, Maryann delivered my Avon brochure with a flyer inside. She had done this so many times in the years before, yet I had never paid much attention to the flyers. However, this time I stopped to look at the recruiting flyer explaining the Avon opportunity. It said I could work Avon around my life for a mere $20. I called her to inquire about it. I did not have time for in-home parties or money to stockpile products. She told me neither was necessary. She asked me to give it six months. I agreed, with the intention to start in April and be out in July, just long enough to pay for my son's needs.

Lee Bibb had come into my life. He became a great friend and support for the boys and me. He was always there to watch them when needed and to listen as I beat myself up for making bad life decisions. I wondered aloud to him when I would get it right. I had never made more than $7.25 an hour and did not know how to dream about more than survival.

Lee asked what my dreams were. This was uncomfortable. I realized I was so busy just making it to the next day that I did not know how to dream. When he asked me to think about something I really wanted, I came up with seeing George Strait in concert and seeing the Dallas Cowboys play in their stadium. Lee took me to my first George Strait concert. My first dream had come true! When he asked, "What's next?" I was afraid to even consider my next dream.

My Avon business started out slowly. My first order was $53. I barely made the commission requirement to make a profit. If I was going to have a graduation party for my son, I had to get some customers. I decided that to make the business work, I would have to incorporate Avon into my life.

I started buying brochures 100 at a time and when I delivered newspapers in the middle of the night I tossed brochures in driveways or put them on top of newspapers in the paper boxes. I waited patiently, and one by one the calls and emails started coming—five new customers! The next night, I did it again and 100 brochures led to seven more customers. I had hit the jackpot and loved it.

> *"You will never reach your goals without a timeline. Until then they are just thoughts and dreams."*
> **—Dave Ramsey, American financial author, radio host, television personality and motivational speaker**

My second order was almost $200 and that amount increased with every order. On expired brochures, I placed labels asking people to call me for current prices and delivered them with newspapers too. People called! Soon, I paid for prom and graduation, I had over fifty customers, and my sales were well over $500 every campaign. Within that first year, I was able to quit my paper route because Avon was more than supplementing my income for that job. I had more time for my kids and I loved selling Avon products.

Approaching Leadership

Maryann and Ray Penn approached me about the leadership program with Avon. When they explained it, I thought *No way, I just like selling it!* They then said that I had the opportunity to make a recruiting bonus of $500. Without hesitation, I was in—$500 sounded like $1 million to me back then. *Show me the money!*

Maryann and Ray said they saw something in me that I never saw in myself—*potential* to be more than I had ever been. It made me uncomfortable to hear them say I could be successful as a leader in Avon. I never saw myself as a leader, as someone who could help change lives. I was just showing people how to do what I did— sharing an Avon brochure.

Love and Money

Lee and I had become much closer and I began to fall in love with him. He was supportive and my biggest cheerleader. However, I was afraid to share Avon with him. The business was my baby, the first thing that ever belonged to me. I was scared to let anyone in on it. I quickly realized after my first Avon President's Club Gala that success by yourself was pretty lonely.

Except for Lee, I had not received much support for my business. Even when I went home with awards after the Gala, most of my family was unsupportive. They asked when I would give up "that little lipstick thingy," which was hurtful and caused self-doubt. They did not understand how much it meant to me. I thought I could really make something of it. Soon I figured out that Avon was helping me to mature into someone they did not recognize. I learned to use their negative remarks and attitudes to push me to say *I'll show you.*

When I made Unit Leader (UL) and the $500 bonus, I was thrilled. Soon my sights were set on Advanced Unit Leader (AUL). My first goal was to fire my boss. I wanted to help people cut through all the crap like I did and find their way to a better life. I wanted to reach financial independence by letting go of the emotional baggage from years of emotional abuse. First I had to prove this could be done.

Almost a year later, I had obtained AUL and Executive Unit Leader (EUL) was on my radar. There was something else on my radar too. Lee had asked me to marry him. I had to figure out how to plan a wedding and reach my goal at the same time. We both had full-time jobs and were working seven days a week. We planned our wedding in the front seat of my car while going after the next goal. I was determined to reach EUL before saying I do.

Eight campaigns later, on my wedding day, I received the official word that I was EUL. While walking down the aisle toward the man I loved, I had another reason to smile. All the hard work and sacrifices had paid off—I got my "E" on!

Tragedy and Triumph

"Life is 10% what happens to you and 90% how you react to it."
—Charles R. Swindoll, American evangelical Christian pastor, author, educator and radio preacher

I would love to say that getting my "S" on and becoming a Senior Executive Unit Leader (SEUL) was an easy journey. However, something I could not control kept getting in the way—life.

I continued working my business every day. I was passionate about Avon and all it had brought into my life. My business was helping me become more confident. For the first time, I was doing something that allowed me to help change lives of men and women everywhere while making a good living.

I traveled many valleys in my quest to make SEUL. My oldest son, Earl, was hurt in a work related accident. He was hit in the eye with a high-powered tool and was rushed to the hospital in Baltimore so that doctors could try to save his eye. All the bones around his eye socket were shattered. The lens in his eye was destroyed and had to be replaced with an artificial lens. I sat with him for days through surgeries and doctor visits.

I could not work my business, yet every two weeks for six weeks, I received my leadership check because my team was working. My customers understood. A light bulb went on in my head that the residual income of my Avon business took care of me and I did not have to lift a finger or worry.

Two years later, while working toward my "S" again, Lee was diagnosed with a degenerative eye disease and there was no cure. We were devastated. He was going blind and I could not fix it. I yelled at God, *Really? Something else? What did I do to deserve this?* We eventually dealt with the challenge and realized it was part of our journey and we were a team. We were going to let nothing get in our way of becoming SEULs.

We soon would figure out just how cruel life could be. Ray Penn was our upline and mentor in Avon, however he had become so much more to Lee and me. He and his wife Maryann were lifetime friends to me, and Ray was like a brother to Lee. The four of us did so much together. Ray had not been feeling well for quite a few months and he was diagnosed with Leukemia. Treatment was to start immediately. We were scared, yet hopeful. He had a great attitude. All he was worried about was their team.

As Ray finished his first treatment of chemotherapy, I suppose his body could not handle the strain and we lost him suddenly. That day will play in my head forever. In the days and months that followed, I supported Maryann as we mourned Ray together. It was another example of how Avon was there for us in so many ways.

These are only a few standout events in my life where, even at the worst of times, I was able to work Avon around my life.

"A good leader is a person who takes a little more than his share of the blame and a little less than his share of the credit."
—John Maxwell, American evangelical Christian author, speaker and pastor

Onward—No Matter What!

In a 2011 Avon meeting, friend and SEUL David Gomez called me out in front of everyone and asked, "Molly, when are you going to get to Senior?" I replied that I was trying. He came right back at me and said, "Molly, when are you going to say, 'No matter what?'" Wow! That was life altering and was the birth of my team motto, "Onward—no matter what!"

Lee and I made a plan and calculated how many people we needed to make SEUL. We decided to take our eyes off of ourselves and help our team reach their goals. That is when things started happening.

We partnered with our soon-to-be Executive Linda Staggers and started working seven days a week toward our goal of helping our team build units. We showed them the money! We partnered with them and watched the numbers pop. We set a goal to make SEUL by Campaign 7 in 2012 and got our "S" on in Campaign 6. Lee was going to see Alaska and the glaciers before his eyesight was gone. This was on his bucket list and for me it felt so good to achieve something we had worked toward for years.

I strive every day to run with the big dogs in Avon. However, God has given Lee and I another purpose in this life: to help representatives all over the country through national conference calls and YouTube® videos. We realized through social media that many people have no direction or support and sometimes just need to hear "Job well done!"

Never think that because of "life" you cannot succeed. I am proof positive that if you keep moving onward you can achieve your dreams and goals no matter what! Above all, never forget that it is about the journey. Do not miss a minute of it—your journey shapes you into who you are meant to be and will be an inspiration to those around you.

MOLLY STONE-BIBB

Avon® Senior Executive Unit Leader
Rose Circle Seller
(800) 868-8812
onward.with.molly@gmail.com
www.facebook.com/groups/onward.
no.matter.what/
www.youtube.com/molly7720

Molly has been a people pleaser since childhood. That character trait has served her well throughout her life. Molly worked as a secretary and delivered newspapers. Despite many challenges, detours and heartbreaks, she started her successful Avon business as a 40-year-old single mother of two boys.

Molly found a love of the Avon opportunity and began her famous journey. She made President's Club and Unit Leader in her first year. Over the following year Molly and her fiancé, Lee, planned a wedding from the front seat of her Avon mobile as they pushed to make Executive Unit Leader. On the day of their wedding in 2005, Molly and Lee made Executive Unit Leader. Today she is a Senior Executive Unit Leader.

Molly works her business around her life full-time and enjoys her role as a mother and wife. The title she wears most proudly is that of grandmother to her beautiful granddaughter, Skylier Elizabeth. Molly happily tells others that her journey was absolutely worth it.

Painting the Canvas of Your Dreams

BY DAN AND JACKIE MUNDY

I was raised on a large dairy farm in Springfield, Ohio. I never had much, yet always had what I needed. I was a child entrepreneur. As a young boy, I sold seed, socks and hosiery, had three newspaper routes, and started my own business selling rides in my homemade "soap box" racer.

Our small town was like a family and most of us were related. From the fifth grade on, I bought my own school clothes and any extra things I wanted. I got one pair of shoes at the beginning of school each year. They wore out by summer time and I went barefoot until school began again. Cardboard was my favorite toy, which I used to slide down hills.

Dairy work was hard. We started early and finished late. Early on, my father instilled in me to work hard. He said, "Whatever is worth doing, it is worth doing right." My youthful days were filled with warm memories and many life-long lessons.

Jackie and I married in 1962 and soon had two daughters. I worked full-time for International Harvester, a company known today as Navistar® International Corporation. At the same time, I taught guitar lessons and drove a semi tractor-trailer hauling nursery stock for my father. The work ethic instilled in me when I was young never left me. Working three jobs was hard, however I believed it was the right thing to do. When our first son was born, I began working part-time with a direct selling company that sold biodegradable products. Our family was complete with the birth of our second son and my business kept growing.

I retired from International Harvester with ten years of service in 1972 to work our direct selling business full-time. Vondell McKenzie had also joined the company and our families built businesses in Ohio. We became good friends and often camped at each other's home.

As a result of our success in building our first direct selling business, the company eventually offered me a position as a national marketing director and we moved to San Jose, California. Jackie and I convinced Vondell and her husband Terry to also move to California. We enjoyed time together again and our families explored the state together, enjoying the wonderful climate.

Our business did not last due to many company changes. The McKenzies joined another company and Jackie and I became disillusioned with direct selling. Our two daughters got married four months apart, which moved me to seek other avenues of work. I became an insurance broker and an estimator for a construction company and we moved to Sacramento, California. Within a month of settling into our new home, the construction company had a major financial upset and that income stopped.

It was time to start over again and we started selling mobile homes. Jackie loved matching people up with affordable housing. At first, we thoroughly enjoyed this, however the market changed in 1990 with a negative impact on the value of mobile homes. Many owners suffered from a loss in value and the financing plans they had embraced became hardships. We experienced a great emotional toll along with the loss of our income and potential. However, we did receive a wonderful gift—our handsome grandson.

While Jackie and I were going through these difficulties, we received a call from Vondell, who felt she had found the right company at the right time. Jackie took the call and what happened next has become one of her favorite stories.

Jackie's Story

Dan was fifty years old and unemployed. He was over qualified and too old for most traditional types of employment. I knew I would have to go to work myself. Vondell called the day before they disconnected our phone. We had not talked in a long time. After catching up on family news, she asked me if Dan would be interested in earning $120,000 a year. I replied that I did not know about Dan, but I would be interested.

Vondell had become an Avon® representative and introduced us to the leadership opportunity. Although Dan's mother supported herself with Avon, he could not see how we could earn the money we needed by selling cosmetics. However, we trusted Vondell because we knew her work ethic and her success in business. Since she thought we could make $120,000, we believed we could!

I was not concerned about the ability to sell products, as three people in a grocery store asked me for an Avon brochure after seeing mine.

I knew then that people wanted Avon. We had little faith at first, yet we knew the products sold.

We called Vondell often and knew where we were going with our new business. We believed in Avon's trusted and respected reputation. Our previous painful experiences had taught us a lot and that pain became an asset once we became Avon representatives. Whenever another representative found it difficult or went through hard times, we understood because we had been there.

Dan was always very focused on whatever he did and now he was focused on building an Avon business. Life was becoming fun again and we enjoyed working with recruits and helping them stay on track.

Dan motivates others and I can motivate him. I love earning prizes and rewards, and Avon provides plenty of incentives. I would ask Dan, *What do you have to do to get me that recognition pin I want? What do you have to do so we can go on that trip?* Traveling has always been a big part of our lives and the best way to travel is to do so for free. When our children were small, we would borrow money to travel just to ensure that their world was always bigger than what they saw every day.

Others enjoy travel too—especially free trips! Therefore, Dan designed incentive trips for our team. Once, we held a contest for a trip with us to Europe. Rebecca (Dorsey) Alejandre and Ann Brito, outstanding representatives whom we had the pleasure of sponsoring, won the trip and Vondell joined us too. Although Rosemarie and Bill Osolinsky met the requirements, they were unable to go. Six of us spent 14 days together. We flew to Paris for a couple of days and then took the Best of France bus tour. We went through Burgundy down to Monte Carlo. We ate at a quaint, little restaurant overlooking the Mediterranean Sea. At the top of one mountain road you could see the azure blue of the Great Sea and the snowcapped Italian Alps on the other side. We stayed in the castle shown in a Saturn® commercial and saw the Roman aqueduct—shown in a Volkswagen® commercial. Our biggest pleasure was having been able to sponsor an incentive trip ourselves and experience the joy in others who won the trip!

From our very first Avon trip, we wanted to share our first-class experiences with our representatives. We feel thankful being part of a company that believes in recognition. We have been able to share this opportunity with many. Over the years, some of them have qualified for the national trips. Seeing them succeed inspires us. We knew they would be successful in whatever they chose to do—and they chose Avon. (See Rosemarie Osolinsky's chapter, *Make Success Attainable: Working Strategically to Grow Quickly* on page 237) Now they, too, touch other people's lives by willingly sharing a part of themselves and putting their heart and soul into it. The respect and love they show us is priceless. Words cannot express our deep feelings of gratitude and joy for the opportunity to work with so many wonderful people. Dan loves talking about the Avon opportunity and will share with you our philosophy.

Our Philosophy

Have a simple plan and reachable steps to make it work—and work hard. Envision the big picture in order to fill in your canvas. From day one, I approached Avon as a full-time career opportunity. I learned the basics and then multiplied my efforts by ten. John Fleming's *Power of 3* became my "Power of 10." Any plan of action is only as good as the consistency of the effort applied. Following through is also key. When you get your momentum going, follow-up has a tendency to fall through the cracks. Consistency with intensity determines the speed of your success!

Our only source of income was Avon, therefore we built our customer base and increased our sales to pay the bills. If we collected cash, it went toward groceries or gas. If we received a check, it went into our Avon checking account to pay the company whatever we owed for the last order. We often had to sell something to put gas in the car to go to an Avon appointment we had scheduled. At the end of a campaign, adding up the total receipts paid by check or cash, for tax purposes, gave us a guide to measure our sales growth and how much money we had to reinvest in our business.

We went from President's Club to Rose Circle to President's Council— our personal sales to customers grew to approximately $100,000 per year. This income allowed us to focus effectively on building our leadership group. Our personal sales success gave us great credibility when we shared with others who also wanted to earn additional income.

In the early days of building our business, succeeding with personal sales was very important. Since our territory was a gated community, we bulk mailed catalogs and followed up using a reverse directory. Jackie suffered frequent migraine headaches, therefore a friend and working buddy helped with the phone calls.

We had one car at that time and therefore utilized our time well. While one of us was at an appointment or with a customer, the other would go to the neighbors with brochures or have an appointment nearby. You can replicate our methods by doing the same thing with one of your serious business-minded representatives. Economize and train simultaneously. We have found that when you look for customers, you also find those wanting to sell, and when you look for someone who wants to sell, you also find customers. They go hand-in-hand.

I have always felt comfortable in an office setting. We had a 140-square-foot office space with four desks, four cabinets, a narrow table and a small space for our baby grandson. Our "Business Development and Career Center" provided our gated community customers with a location to visit. As our business grew, our office became more professional.

Take pride in your appearance, products and business opportunities. Be ready for any occasion that might present itself. Even when I worked from home, I got up every morning and dressed ready for work, always looking presentable to anyone I might come in contact with. Jackie always looked professional too. She prepared several well put-together business outfits, including black skirts and slacks along with black, white, or red blouses, jackets, sweaters and accessories.

While Jackie and I performed our daily activities, we sought out serious business-minded people. She looked for people wanting to make a little extra money, while her mission was to find people who wanted to buy Avon and had lost their representative in the Sacramento area.

Do your homework to maximize your opportunities. I focus on what the company has to offer. When Avon was forming the leadership opportunity, I created additional incentives to grow our unit. Today, Avon provides us with a lot to work with.

Keep your lines of communication open. Avon has increased avenues of communication for representatives. In an ever-changing world of technology, utilize every aspect you can to improve your business. It has always been a challenge for me to talk before a group. E-communications helped me to reach many people at once.

To point your downline representatives in the right direction, understand where they are and where they want to go. Help them find the solutions that work in accordance with their goals and plans. They can find everything they need in Avon's Pathways. Keep it simple! Help them see the big picture as you paint yours.

Painting the canvas of your dreams starts with a written, long-term goal. Fill in the canvas by planning reachable steps. Pause to determine your next layer of goals and steps and repeat that until you are ready for the final details. The fluid properties of oil paints allow the artist to make corrections. Therefore, when life or business throws you a curve, quickly readjust your goals to meet your needs. The more flexible you are in working your short-term goals, the more definition your long-term goal will have—more color, more life. You can have a masterpiece!

Living the Dream

Avon has been great for us. It has allowed us to travel. The national trip to Hawaii in 2013 was a highlight in our business career. We flew first-class and upon our arrival on the island, a private limousine took us to the hotel where a fruit basket awaited us. From our room overlooking the ocean, we had a beautiful view of Diamond Head. As usual, the events were spectacular. Many representatives of our Nova team also experienced this wonderful trip. Some were with us when we first received recognition at a national event. Best of all, some receive recognition now at national events for their successes and accomplishments. Being a part of this is a great privilege.

Avon has also allowed us to return to country living. The house—Jackie got to go with her first written goal, a refrigerator—was replaced with a custom-built cottage in the woods. We now live on an 89-acre farm in rural Illinois with our son, daughter, son-in-law and grandson. They live close at hand in the refurbished farmhouse. (Our youngest son's marriage brought us a new daughter-in-law and a lovely granddaughter who still live in California.)

Only 20 acres are farmed and the rest of the property is wooded hills with a creek flowing through. Our two goats keep us entertained and relaxed as we watch them jump around and play. We enjoy entertaining around our 2-acre pond with hayrides, bonfires and riding our John Deere® "gator" on the trails through the woods. We truly appreciate our new home and thoroughly enjoy watching our friends and our children's friends enjoying themselves.

I have a collection of guitars and my favorite is from Jackie. I learned to play finger style because Jackie likes soft music and enjoys it when I play late in the evening as I unwind.

The person who first introduced me to direct selling quoted the common saying, "There are those people who make things happen, and others who watch things happen, while others wonder what has happened." This made a big impression on me. Be the one to make things happen. Be the driver of the bus, not the rider. Be the one going somewhere, not just going along watching things pass by. Be consistent with intensity and do not give up.

Remember your big picture. Set your paints out, make an outline, prepare your canvas, and start painting your dreams. Now is the time to fill in your canvas, from the wispy shadow of the background to the clear-cut image in the foreground. Make things happen.

Much Success to you!

DAN AND JACKIE MUNDY

Avon® Senior Executive Unit Leaders

avonasap@aol.com
www.youravon.com/danmundy

Married since 1962, Dan and Jackie now live in rural Illinois. Dan retired from International Harvester after ten years of service, has run various businesses, and has over forty years direct selling experience. He and Jackie began building their Avon business in 1991. Dan and Jackie earned Senior Executive Unit Leader (SEUL) status in 1992, right after their sponsor Vondell McKenzie did, making them the first second-generation SEUL in Avon.

Dan and Jackie have been recognized at National Events and consistently been in the top five of the nation with Avon. In 2013, they were number two in the nation for Leadership Total Unit Sales and number one in the nation for Leadership Sales Increase. Their "history makers and record breakers" team filled three of the four top national leadership positions.

Dan and Jackie live in a custom-built cottage in a tranquil wooded setting and enjoy spending time with their children and grand-children. They take pleasure in unwinding to the sound of Dan playing music on his guitar in the evenings.

Transformation at Its Best

BY LAURA DOUGLAS-ROBINSON

How does a once shy, young woman from Harlem become an officer in the largest police department in the world—the New York Police Department (NYPD)—retire as a young sergeant after twenty years of service, and then become one of the top level leaders of Avon®—a Senior Executive Unit Leader (SEUL)? The first word that comes to mind is determination.

I have come a long way from being shy and quiet. I was the one who was always the tallest girl in class, the one who had to stand in the back of the line, and who just wanted to hide.

I was the oldest of four children. My parents married young and, of course, I was the one who was given the responsibility of being the second mommy. Little did I know that this was a blessing in disguise because I learned leadership skills very early. My mother always treated me like her right arm and depended on me to help her. She always considered me the example for my siblings. Words cannot express how close to my mother I was. She instilled in me the power to be the best at whatever I decided to do. My parents made me want to be successful.

At the age of 18, I took the police test and informed my parents that I wanted to be a police officer. They were both shocked because I was shy and because I had wanted to be a psychiatrist. I do not think I fell too far away from that goal. The thought of spending eight more years in school quickly changed my mind about being a psychiatrist. I really felt the need to help people. I loved action and thought police work was more for me.

The First Transformation — My Life Changes Forever

My problem with being shy and quiet quickly went away once I entered the police academy. What a way to knock the shyness out of you! I had to make a change and try to get out of my comfort zone. I knew I was destined to go far in life. It begins with me. My mother was right beside me with a dose of courage when needed. She could not let me fail and I could not let myself fail. Graduation came and there I was on patrol in Manhattan.

My Shyness Disappears Forever

Working on patrol in the city of New York can quickly take the shyness out of you. During my first few weeks on a foot post in Manhattan, I encountered a woman who was badly beaten by two accomplices. She was covered in blood from head to toe and near death. I was the lucky one who came upon the scene and assisted her. I eventually arrested the culprits. Another day, I was in a police car and was the lucky one again to receive a call about a bank robbery.

The robber was still there and was quickly arrested without further incident. I have seen all kinds of crimes and many situations that you could not imagine seeing in a lifetime.

The Second Transformation—from Officer to Sergeant

Being a sergeant in the NYPD gave me invaluable skills to use for the rest of my life. What happened to the shy girl from Harlem? She was gone forever. I was now the one who was responsible for directing other officers in their duties. I was the first line of supervision and was summoned to make decisions without hesitation. I was a sergeant at the age of 26, telling officers—some of whom were old enough to be my father—what to do.

There were very few women where I worked. In order for me to be successful, I had to earn respect from my officers. I had to show confidence to gain their trust. We handled life and death situations. There was no time to show any lack of confidence. I had to be prepared no matter what. I survived 14 years as a supervisor out of my twenty-year career. I used one of the keys to success—determination. My goal was to become a supervisor and to retire at forty years old, and I reached that goal. There was nothing left I could face that would give me a challenge—or so I thought!

The Third Transformation Begins—Avon

I had started selling Avon in high school as a hobby. I felt it was a great way to meet people and earn extra money. However, I had let it go to pursue a police career. I met my future husband Gilbert Sr. soon after being assigned to my first precinct. He was chosen to be my partner in the patrol car. We became very close and many years later, we fell in love and got married.

I started Avon again, and detoured again being newly married and wanting to start a family. I always dreamed of having boys, like my father's mother. I was blessed to have two of them. They are two and a half years apart; therefore I had somewhat of a break from breastfeeding and diapers between them. I decided to work the "graveyard shift" until I retired because I wanted to feel like a full-time mother. I always felt tired, yet it was worth it being home during the day and becoming very involved in their education.

Getting close to retirement, I was now the mother of two boys, homeowner, and still fairly young. I have always loved the idea of being a representative of Avon. I tried other businesses such as Tupperware® and Quixtar® (Amway® Global). However, Avon always superseded them.

In 2000, I returned to Avon and have never thought of leaving again. I made good money selling and reached the top seller status soon thereafter. The following year, I achieved the first level of leadership.

I retired from the police department in 2002 and was free to be a full-time mother and devote more time to my Avon business. I spent a lot of time attending seminars and meetings. I wanted to make sure I learned everything in order to reach the higher pay levels. You have to make time and give 100 percent in order to see results.

My best motivators and upline, Maria and Donald Tirotta, helped me in every way to keep me going. Their inspirational story of making Avon their full-time business and being successful, kept me close to them. To say I was challenged to reach their level is an understatement. I stayed at the first level of leadership for seven years. I could not move to the next level. What was holding me back?

The Final Transformation—the Road to the Top

My dreams of being a top-level leader quickly came to light again when I received a phone call from my then district manager, Bozena Grabowski. I believe Bozena is one of the best district managers the company has. She is in a class by herself. She came at a time in my life when I needed to make a change. I knew what I wanted, and I just needed someone to help me get out of my "police attitude."

> *"It is not your aptitude, but your attitude,*
> *that determines your altitude."*
> **—Zig Ziglar, American author, salesman**
> **and motivational speaker**

Bozena congratulated me on my great selling status and also made me realize that my skills as a leader in Avon were stagnant. How did she do that? She pointed out my small checks, which were nothing to boast about. Bozena was what I needed. Someone who was not afraid to tell me like it is. When I told her that I did not think it was my fault that I was stuck, right away she disagreed with me. What was I lacking?

What Skills Did I Lack?

- I was afraid to approach strangers. You must do the prospecting to build your team.
- I feared rejection. Always be positive.
- I did not know how to train and develop my team. You must coach and cultivate your team.
- I lacked the ability to build relationships with my team. Be a friend first, and then a leader to your team.
- I could not put away my police sergeant skills. Be optimistic for change. Allow yourself to be trainable. Come with a clean slate.

There I was, a retired police sergeant, yet I was afraid to approach strangers. I was only used to approaching strangers while in uniform. I needed a lot of help. I had to revert back to being a civilian, which was difficult for me. First, I had to believe I could change.

Another key to success is to *believe in yourself.* Being a police officer transforms you. You are taught to always be on guard. You are constantly looking for something to happen. While everyone around you is enjoying themselves, you are watching the doors, checking everyone out. It becomes a way of life. They say, "Once a cop, always a cop." I needed to tone it down if I wanted to be successful in a networking business. Somehow Bozena understood what I was going through. We clicked right away and she committed herself to helping me. We spent many hours, days and months getting me out of my guarded personality. It worked! The new me emerged and this transformation was complete.

10 Ways to Be a True Leader

1. Believe in yourself. Confidence is very much needed.

2. Be positive, always. Never show negativity.

3. Be open-minded. Do not close your mind to new learning.

4. Be a Leader—not a follower.

5. Be an example of what you expect from others.

6. Be remembered for what you do, not what you tell others to do. Show and tell, not tell and not show.

7. Be able to look in the mirror and truly say that you are doing all you can to help others achieve their dreams.

8. Be committed to your team.

9. Be available with your time.

10. Be focused, always.

I learned these strategies from Bozena Grabowski and Maria and Donald Tirotta, the network marketing way. They are not in any particular order and I encourage you to master them all.

Once I applied these leadership strategies to my business, it went to a whole different level. In the first six months of working with Bozena, I advanced my title. I had to let go of my inhibitions and open myself up to learning what I was lacking. Do not be afraid to change. The road to the top requires changes in your life.

I had to make sure my family understood that my many hours away from home would be well worth it when I achieved my dream of being financially independent. This endeavor was for them as much as it was for me. With that, you must make some sacrifices.

My two children are now young men. They grew up at the right time for me to be able to spend more time out of the house. It helped that my husband and I were both retired. I was free as a bird to devote my time to Avon. I still had to be at home sometimes, so I had to carve a schedule with them.

My life as an Avon representative became my full-time job—and I became my own boss. It is a great feeling to come and go as I please. I intend to make $10,000 a month. This requires work and I am halfway there. Set aside your goal and plan your action. It did not happen in a day, but look what happened to me once I applied myself in the right direction. The fact that it was not easy makes me appreciate it that much more.

I have more than 18 trophies and awards for Top Recruiter, Sales Growth and other recognitions. I have earned several trips, including Alaska, Hawaii and Las Vegas. I have participated in many panel groups and studies and have represented Avon at many social events.

I believe things happen for a reason. It was my time to make a change. I am grateful that I did not give up and stayed with the company I love. My family has told me many times that they are proud that I held onto my dreams. I am sure they do not mind the extra money!

Surround yourself with positive people. Being around positive people is contagious and well worth the company. Spend time with the people with whom you have common goals. I continue to learn from my peers. You never know everything. At least the smart ones know that.

> *"Magic is believing in yourself. If you can do that,*
> *you can make anything happen."*
> **—Johann Wolfgang Von Goethe, German writer**
> **and politician**

In 2012, I fulfilled my dream of achieving SEUL, the top level in Avon, and my unit sales reached over one million dollars. Words cannot express my gratitude to Maria and Donald Tirotta for their never-ending efforts to motivate me to *never give up*. They are loved more than they could ever know. I am also truly grateful to Bozena Grabowski, who showed me how to change and become a true leader in Avon. She will forever be my best friend and coach, and loved like a sister to me.

My story is dedicated to my mother Esther Douglas. She is now gone, yet will forever remain in my heart. She made me stand tall and proud. I thank her for being there for me. Until we meet again.

Now you have seen how I, like so many others, had to make changes within myself. We went around the obstacles, jumped over them, pushed them out of the way, and did whatever we needed to do to reach our goals. We all have inhibitions; just do not allow them to get in your way. Believe in yourself. Give your dreams a chance to be achieved. You will be very happy to say to yourself *I did it!*

LAURA DOUGLAS-ROBINSON

Avon® Senior Executive Unit Leader
Honor Society-Spirit of Avon
Avon Eagles
Change is good
917-885-8639
sgtbuster@aol.com
www.youravon.com/ldouglasrobinso

Laura Douglas-Robinson grew up in Harlem, New York. She started her career in law enforcement right after high school. Laura became a police sergeant in 1988 and in the same year, received a degree in forensic psychology from John Jay College of Criminal Justice. She is retired from the New York Police Department.

Laura attended Teacher's College for a while and plans to return. She always dreamed of being a full-time mother to her two boys. The desire to have a second career inspired Laura to become a successful Avon sales leader. She overcame her issues of having a "cop personality" while selling lipstick and became a Senior Executive Unit Leader with Avon New York.

Laura's key to success is to never give up—keep going until you achieve your dream. She continues to help and motivate others to succeed. Laura enjoys travelling and music. She wants to explore the world. Europe and Africa are on her list. She believes travelling the world gives you the education that textbooks cannot teach. Laura continues to donate Avon and money to many charities to further spread the word that she and Avon cares.

Where the Lord Leads

BY PAULA WEATHERLY

"The Lord says, 'I will guide you along the best pathway for your life. I will advise you and watch over you.'"
Psalm 32:8

I am a woman of God. That is the most important part of my Avon® Story. Being a Christian wife and mother defines who I am and the choices I make. Serving Jesus first and foremost is the reason I joined Avon in 2005. It was never in *my* plan, it was always in *His*.

Life has a funny way of leading you down a path you would never choose for yourself. Growing up, I always wanted to have "Dr." preceding my name. However, by the time I graduated from Texas A & M University in 1997, my dream of being a doctor was happily exchanged for a wedding ring.

I married Colin Weatherly and worked various jobs to help make ends meet. I was unfulfilled by my work and always felt I could do more. Lauren was born in 1999 and my heart broke at the thought of leaving my baby to go to work. The Lord provided a job working at a taekwondo school. During the day, the school was closed and I brought Lauren with me. Working there cultivated a love of teaching deep within me. I adored the students and when I watched the impact the instructors had on them, I wanted to make that difference in someone else's life. I felt a calling into a classroom—somewhere I had never dreamed I would be!

I had always wanted to use my gifts and talents to help inspire others to reach their fullest potential. In the fall of 2000, I was hired to teach science at a local high school. Fear is walking into a classroom full of teenagers while being the ripe old age of 25! However, I loved teaching. I loved being a positive role model.

In 2002, our son, Luke, was born. It was still difficult to leave my babies while I worked, however quitting my job to stay at home with them was not an option. After three years of teaching high school, I took a job at a middle school that was much closer to home. I feel like this was the Lord's first push to get me where He designed me to be. Biblically, women are created to be mothers, wives and caregivers. We are supposed to be at home raising our children, yet society has led us away from that. I knew that I should be at home with my kids, yet I also loved my job. God wired me to want to work.

As my kids grew, they needed me at home more and more. In the fall of 2004, I began teaching part-time and thought that I had found the perfect balance between motherhood and career. Unfortunately, the part-time schedule only lasted one year. In May 2005, just after discovering I was pregnant with our third child, I was asked to come back to work full-time. I decided to resign instead.

Choosing Avon to Fit My Life

As you can imagine, life was a little chaotic. Worry about the future filled my husband and me. However, we felt the Lord was telling us to have faith and follow Him. Our bank account was screaming to us that we were nuts to walk away from employment! My mother-in-law, Linda Weatherly, had sold Avon when her kids were little. Colin suggested that I sign up to start selling as soon as possible while we tried to figure out how we were going to live on one income. On June 6, 2005, a district sales manager came to my house and appointed me as a new Avon representative.

I joined Avon because it was just $10 to start and did not require having parties. The result of that decision is mind boggling to me. Who knew that I was destined to be an Avon Lady?

My initial Avon appointment was three hours long. I asked many questions, bought all the brochures the manager had in his car, and tried to grasp the concept of how I was going to start this business and replace my income. I was amazed when I watched the *Rich and Famous of Avon* Volume 2 DVD. The people on the video made lots of money! I did not know that it was possible to make a six-figure income with Avon.

I was unstoppable. I read everything I could find and learned as much as I could. I launched a grand opening by sending emails to everyone in my contact list and hosting a party at my house.

I was moving too quickly for my manager to keep up; therefore he partnered me with another local representative, Jean Fowler. She helped mentor me and because she was working in the trenches too, knew how to answer my questions. She shared information with me and helped calm my fears about backorders and goals. I needed to sell $500 per campaign to make President's Club and vowed that I would reach that first goal.

"Always be joyful. Never stop praying. Be thankful in all circumstances, for this is God's will for you who belong to Christ Jesus."
1 Thessalonians 5:16-18

Overcoming Self Doubt

My world stopped on June 24, 2005. At a routine 12-week doctor visit, my obstetrician could not find our baby's heartbeat. I was flooded with the devastation of losing our child—the baby we had tried to conceive for almost a year and who was my justification for walking away from my teaching career. I began questioning my decision to quit my job.

After much prayer and many tears, we decided I would stay the course and not ask for my teaching job back. I believe everything happens for a reason and I was where God wanted me—at home.

I continued to work relentlessly to build my customer base and sales team. My manager had introduced me to the Leadership program. He told me that with my background in teaching, it would be a great avenue for me to continue teaching others. I recruited friends from my scrapbooking club as my first team members, along with a cousin and a former coworker. I managed to earn the Fast Start Bonus money and realized that leadership was the way to replace my full-time income. From that point forward, I recruited first and sold second.

Success Tips for New Representatives

- **Learn everything you can about the business.** You are a business owner and there is a lot to learn. Master one product per campaign and learn to sell it to all your customers. By the end of one year, you will know how to effectively sell 26 products. The more you learn, the more you earn!

- **Earn Avon's incentives.** Do not leave money on the table. If an incentive is offered, plan how you will earn every penny of it.
- **Remember that your success is up to you.** If you need ideas or have questions that your upline or manager cannot help you with, reach out to others for guidance. We have all been where you are— new, excited, confused and overwhelmed. Do not give up, because you can be successful!

"Work hard and cheerfully at whatever you do, as though you were working for the Lord rather than for people. Remember that the Lord will give you an inheritance as your reward, and the Master you are serving is Christ."
Colossians 3:23-24

My team needed a name. It was God's prompting that had lead me to Avon, therefore I chose "Amazing Grace Avon Team" in honor of my favorite hymn. I wanted to give God the honor and glory in everything related to my new business. I used the above Colossians verse as the Mission Statement for our team.

I was met with criticism for my choice of team names. One of my first team members asked to be removed from my email list because I included Bible verses in every email. This did not sway me. In fact, I started viewing my Avon business as more than just a way to make money. It was also a way to minister to others.

No matter what brings people to your Avon team, they all share one common trait—they need someone to love them, appreciate them, and reassure them that they are important. I could do that for each of them! I might not be able to solve all their problems, however I could be a listening ear, a shoulder to cry on, or a high-five for their success.

My district sales manager, Dusty Johnson, taught me that there are not that many "atta-girls" in this life. I could be a cheerleader for these team members and be a positive influence in their lives.

Life's Joys Combined with Business

Although it was not easy, I worked persistently over the next few years to build my business. The Lord blessed us with another child, just a few months after my miscarriage. I gave birth to Landon in May of 2006, on the day of my very first President's Club Tribute! I missed the luncheon for obvious reasons, yet was awarded Best New Performer for my district. In addition to a trophy for my hard work, I held a precious baby in my arms knowing I was indeed doing the work that God had planned for my life—to be at home raising my family.

I promoted to Advanced Unit Leader in 2007. I had been in business for over 18 months and I finally started seeing the real fruits of my labor. My division manager, Beth Samples, had regularly scheduled top leader meetings for our area. These meetings inspired me. I received recognition for my achievements and felt appreciated. After being at home with laundry, dishes and diapers, it was great to feel like I was making a difference.

By that time, I had recruited a couple of big "go-getters" to my team. Working with them, I moved to the rank of Executive Unit Leader (EUL). I could not be more excited about my future with Avon.

Tips for Advancing

- **Look for volunteers.** Do not drag people into leadership with you or you will drag them throughout their Avon career. This wears you out physically and mentally. Look for people who are willing to work to make their business successful because they want it for themselves.

- **Talk to more people.** A continuous influx of additional people joining your team helps maintain your current title and helps you advance. I count each representative as $100. If you are trying to make Unit Leader and the sales requirement is $1200, you will need at least 12 people on your team to achieve stability (12 X $100 = $1200). The same is true for the upper ranks. You can advance with fewer people, however the more you have, the easier it is to consistently hit your campaign goals.
- **Set goals.** It is hard to get to your destination without a map. Have a plan and work diligently to accomplish it. Decide how many people each day you will talk to about your business. Set a goal for the minimum number of new recruits you will appoint each campaign. Setting goals is vital for your business. Help your new team members set goals as well—when they reach their goals, it helps you to reach yours too!

I wish I could say that I quickly moved from EUL to Senior Executive Unit Leader (SEUL), however that is not the case. Early in 2010, my top leader decided to step down from the business. It was a devastating blow. I lived in denial for months thinking that she would be back. After all, we had become close friends and were true business partners. Over the next year, I felt the pains of going backward instead of forward in my business. I dropped title from EUL back to Unit Leader.

"Commit your actions to the LORD,
and your plans will succeed."
Proverbs 16:3

In 2011, Avon announced some major changes to the Leadership program. They introduced the Nesting program and changed the requirements for title advancement. Suddenly, reaching the top level of SEUL was within my reach again. More determined than ever, I resolved to maximize the Nesting program and laid out a plan to reach Senior, which I achieved in 2012. It was not an easy road to the top, however I found much joy in the journey.

Tips for Staying on Course

- **Realize the path will have bumps and turns along the way.** Expect them and resolve not to quit no matter how big the roadblock.
- **Reward yourself for meeting small goals.** Celebrate your successes when you reach each milestone on your journey. Recognize your team members and praise them when they reach their goals. Celebration is a great motivator—do not forget this part of the process.
- **Remember the power of prayer.** I have spent so much time in prayer for my business over the years—prayers for my team members and for my decision-making. I have prayed that I will be used as a blessing to others. When the Lord is with you, all things are possible.

I cannot imagine my life without Avon. I have replaced my teaching income and plan to earn six figures. The time I have spent at home raising my children is priceless. I am building a business that can remain in our family for generations.

Freedom, Rewards and Giving Back

In 2013, I earned three trips with Avon. I celebrated a second honeymoon in Jamaica with my husband. We met friends there who have become like family to us. I earned a trip to Las Vegas and enjoyed a private Bon Jovi concert! My first annual awards trip was to Hawaii—something I had wanted to do my entire life. Years of hard work building the business has paid off tremendously.

I have participated in the Avon Walk for Breast Cancer since 2008. This is a life-changing weekend in which I encourage you to participate. Nothing has made me prouder than to see our company name associated with such a powerful event. The Avon Foundation for Women has a positive impact in the lives of so many! From looking for a cure for breast cancer to putting an end to domestic violence, I am proud to be a part of this company that values the lives of others. There are nine Avon Walks around the country every year. I challenge you to do something to be involved with one of them. Whether it is raising at least $1800 and walking the 39.3 miles over the weekend, helping your local walkers fundraise, or cheering for the walkers, you will be blessed by your participation in this event.

> *"Never be lazy, but work hard and*
> *serve the Lord enthusiastically."*
> **Romans 12:11**

There is no magical formula to achieve business success. Everyone has a different story about his or her journey to the top. I believe there is only one common denominator between them—hard work and perseverance. Never give up. Set your goals and aim high. The only people who fail at this business are those who quit. Aspire to reach your goals and exceed your wildest dreams. We only have one life to live here on this Earth. Make every day count!

PAULA WEATHERLY

Avon® Senior Executive Unit Leader
Honor Society Member
Amazing Grace Avon Team
(713) 515-2299
paulaweatherly97@gmail.com
www.shopwithpaula.net
www.agavonteam.wordpress.com

Paula is a Christian wife and mother of three. After graduating from Texas A & M University, she taught science for five years. Paula realized her calling was to be at home raising her children. She launched her Avon business in 2005 and has risen to the top leadership level of the company.

Paula was named the Best New Performer for her district during her first year in business. She has achieved numerous recruiting and team building awards and several incentive trips. In 2006 and 2013, Paula received the prestigious Spirit of Avon Award. She views her business as a ministry and believes that anyone can be successful in Avon if they work hard and do not give up. Avon gives her an opportunity to witness to and mentor others to achieve their fullest potential. Paula believes that changing lives for the better has value that will last into eternity.

Paula volunteers in the youth group at her church and serves on the board of Captivated by God Ministries. She participates in the Avon Walk for Breast Cancer Houston every year and encourages others to get involved with the event.

It Started with a Dream

BY CLAUDETTE AND MURTAIN HASKIN

Growing up, I attended a Catholic elementary school and junior high school. I enjoyed the Girl Scouts®, starting as a Daisy and participating all the way to Cadette. I loved being creative and took art classes at the Brooklyn Museum and sewing classes at the YWCA. For my first summer job, at age 14, I taught arts and crafts at a preschool.

Every summer, I went to stay with my paternal family on a farm in Timmonsville, South Carolina. There, I learned all about farm life—chickens, pigs and cows.

As a teenager, I visited with my maternal family in Harbour View, Jamaica, during summer vacation. This experience taught me how people can make a nice, small home with very little money. I learned to grow delicious mangos and ackees, a fruit that looks like a peach. I graduated from the High School of Art and Design in New York, New York.

As a young woman, I always had a flair for fashion and beauty. In the 1970's, I was accepted into the Fashion Institute of Technology (FIT), one of the pre-eminent colleges in the country for style and design. Matriculated as a fashion buying and merchandising major, I took courses in a variety of subjects, including marketing, sales and promotion. I complemented my educational development by working in various retail positions, including one as an assistant buyer at a major department store.

In one of my unique jobs, I worked as an ice skating guard at an upscale rink in Manhattan, where I was responsible for assisting those who were injured to the first aid office. After earning my associate's degree, I enrolled in the University of New Haven, and graduated with a bachelor of science degree in business management.

In the summer of 1978, I met my husband, Murtain, a young medical student who attended a professional school in Washington, D.C. In his youth, Murtain had taken karate and achieved a brown belt. He played basketball at Tilden High School in Brooklyn, New York, from which he graduated. During summer vacations, Murtain visited his paternal family in Virginia.

A few years later, Murtain and I married and were blessed with two identical twin daughters, Latoya and Turquoise. A third daughter, Crystal, added to our joy a couple of years later. During their early years, I decided to be a homemaker so that I could maintain a strong presence during their critical stages of development.

I had always wanted to take my husband on a vacation to St. Thomas, Virgin Islands. I recall viewing a newspaper ad for Avon® representatives. Oddly, I had never sold for a multilevel home-based business, yet I'd always had a dream to start a business with this company! The following day, I purchased the Daily News and was delighted to see another ad for Avon. I responded to the advertisement and an Avon associate contacted me to schedule an appointment at a local office in Brooklyn, New York.

While there were many home business opportunities on the market, I decided that it would be ideal to work for a company with brand recognition, great support, a stellar reputation, premium products that were attractive to consumers, and an affordable enrollment fee. I found that Avon had all these attributes and signed up as a representative.

The district sales manager suggested I generate a list of fifty potential customers and drop off "What's New" bags door-to-door in a five-block radius from my home. I immediately took action by calling prospective customers and engaging in neighborhood canvassing. I also went through my entire personal telephone book to organize a home demo and sales party. I invited approximately 81 personal contacts and was delighted to greet 39 guests at the gathering. This event served as a launch pad for my success in sales.

As I continued to seek ways to increase my customer base, Murtain offered to drive me to customers' homes to make deliveries, pick up boxes from my local office, and take me to appointments to sign up prospects. Although Murtain had a very tight work schedule, he supported my growing business.

While he never had his own home-based business, he was introduced to network marketing one summer as an assistant to his father who worked as a chef at an exclusive restaurant in a Gramercy Park hotel in New York City. Murtain recalled an occasion when he was washing dishes, and he overheard a coworker discuss the freedom of working from home. Although he was training to heal the sick, the idea of owning a home-based business sounded empowering and had always sparked his interest.

Through our hard work and partnership, I elevated to President's Club—which in the 1980's was the achievement of earning approximately $8,500 in annual sales—within my first year. I was elated by this promotion as I received my first Mrs. Albee Award, earned a minimum forty percent sales commission, could order three discounted demos each campaign, and received an invitation to the exclusive President's Club recognition ceremony. Subsequently, I was able to treat my husband to a dream vacation to St. Thomas, Virgin Islands!

Sustaining the momentum, I accelerated to Honor Society status the following year. I continued to build my customer base and elevated to Rose Circle and McConnell Club, which honors representatives for achieving annual sales of $66,500.

During my fifth year, we moved to Queens, New York, to purchase a larger home, as our children got older. After the move, I set an aggressive goal to attain President's Council, an elite group with $100,000 in annual sales. Motivated by an incentive to earn a vacation to Los Angeles, I engaged my helpers by giving them bonuses for their stellar performance, organized home parties for my customers, and attended exhibitions at fairs and shows. I also sold to the mothers at my daughters' school.

My focus was superior service, fast delivery and excellent product knowledge. As I balanced my five-day work week with parenting my children, I was thrilled to ultimately reap the fruits of my labor—I achieved President's Council, earned a fabulous recognition trip, and 3,000 spending points.

Promotion to District Sales Manager

I continued to perform well at the President's Council level. One day, Allen Winton, my divisional manager, approached me at an

Avon meeting to congratulate me on my sales excellence, money management skills, and recruitment of new representatives for "Starshares," a program which allowed one to convert points into gifts. At the conclusion of our discussion, he requested a copy of my resume. After undergoing a series of interviews, including one at the Newark, Delaware, branch, I was offered an Avon district sales manager position. I was initially undecided because I enjoyed selling at shows and fairs. My district sales manager, Guadalupe Sanchez, encouraged me to accept the position, and I did.

> *"Fear is that little darkroom in your head where your negatives are developed."*
> **—Burton Brown, Jr., American businessman and cancer survivor**

As a district sales manager, I served in more of a leadership capacity. I learned that it is sometimes challenging to motivate others to reach their true potential. I realize now that the greatest limitations to your success are the conscious and subconscious constraints of your thoughts. Some people, perhaps unconsciously, do not feel that they deserve to be prosperous.

We have been blessed with this life and what we do with it—our decisions, resolve and tenacity—determines our prosperity. My husband and I emphasize to our children and others that they can achieve whatever their minds conceive. We encourage you to identify ways to assist people because your success is ultimately a reflection of the service you provide to others. This principle rings true with Avon—the only way you can achieve and be successful is by helping others.

> *"Helping others is the only way we help ourselves."*
> **-Oprah Winfrey, American media proprietor, talk show host, actress, producer and philanthropist**

During my 14-year tenure as a district sales manager, I achieved Circle of Excellence—district sales managers who rank in the top ten percent in the nation for sales increases—on multiple occasions, and I earned incentive trips to Munich, Barcelona, Brussels, Amsterdam, Austria, the Bahamas, Hawaii and areas within the continental United States.

Leaping from Adversity

In 2003, my mother passed, and my grandmother died a few months later. Their deaths marked a very painful period in my life. I was fortunate to have support, understanding and encouragement from my husband and daughters. Through deep reflection, I realized that I still enjoyed working for Avon, yet wanted a more flexible schedule. Therefore I sought new income generating opportunities. After much discussion with my husband, I made the decision to retire from my district sales manager position and enter the recruitment realm by entering the Avon leadership program.

Many of the top leaders on the Avon's Rich and Famous DVD have inspired me. Upon making this transition, I immediately pursued the highest level of leadership, Senior Executive Unit Leader (SEUL). To realize this goal, I developed a ninety-day action plan with Mary Poinson, my district sales manager. I incorporated her suggestions to field prospects three times per week and to create a master list of my personal contacts. It was a long, bumpy five-year road that led me to reach SEUL in 2010.

It is vital that you persevere when confronted with new challenges, keep your eye on the prize, reinvent yourself, and hone your planning and money management skills. It is also important to disregard the naysayers and surround yourself with successful people.

My 600-plus team members, who have produced more than $2 million in sales, have reaped major rewards with their earnings. Here are some of their results:

- Purchased new cars
- Supplemented their job income
- Bought new clothes
- Took family vacations
- Donated to their churches
- Saved money
- Paid for private school education

What other home-based business can you start from the comfort of your home for only $10 and develop it into a six-figure income? Being able to work from home is a dream come true!

"A goal should scare you a little and excite you a lot."
—Joe Vitale, American entrepreneur, self-help author and singer

Achieving Self-Improvement

Being with Avon has definitely changed me as a person. Over time, I developed more confidence and enhanced my public speaking skills and ability to solve business dilemmas. It is essential to have ongoing communication with your team by way of conference calls, in person one-on-one coaching, group e-mails, and postcards. Consider adopting the following skills as you walk down the road to success:

- Return phone calls, texts and emails promptly.
- Promote your Avon website.
- Take advantage of training available at www.youravon.com.
- Be a T.E.A.M. (Together Everyone Achieves More).
- Enroll in Avon's savings plan.
- Be passionate.

- Do not believe the naysayers.
- Be coachable.

Yes, you can have it all!

Books and DVDs I Recommend:
- *The Secret,* by Rhonda Byrne, Atria Books, 2006
- *Fired up!,* by Snowden McFall, Success Publishers, 1997
- *If They Say No,* by John Fuhrman, Possibility Press, 2000
- *Accelerated Success,* by Donna Reid Mitchel
- *A View from the Top, Volume I,* by 25 SEULs Thrive Publishing, 2012
- *The Four Agreements,* by Don Miguel Ruiz, Amber-Allen Publishing, Inc., 1997

Motivational and Spiritual Speakers I Recommend:
- John Maxwell
- TD Jakes
- Les Brown
- Jeffrey Combs
- Joel Osteen
- Stedman Graham

On a personal note, I am very grateful that I had the opportunity to be surrounded by loved ones who supported my success, including my late parents, Frederick and Marilyn McPherson; my late grandmother, Lillian Smith; my in-laws, Essie Haskin and the late Murtain Haskin, Sr.

> *"You were born to win, but to be a winner, you must plan to win, prepare to win, and expect to win!"*
> **—Zig Ziglar, American author, salesman and motivational speaker**

Now that you have read my story, I encourage you to try some of the strategies and discover what works for you. Imagine the life you would love to live, plan your goals, and execute to achieve them. Here is to your success!

CLAUDETTE AND MURTAIN HASKIN
Avon® Senior Executive Unit Leaders

(800) 206-0799
propeL92@aol.com
www.youravon.com/chaskin
www.propeL92.com
Twitter: propeL92com

Raised in Brooklyn, New York, the families of Claudette and Murtain Haskin instilled strong values, emphasized education, and nurtured their talents. These successful role models have been married since 1980, have three professional daughters, and live in Jamaica Estates, New York.

Before graduating from college in Connecticut, Claudette knew she wanted to start her own business. Avon was the right fit for a young wife and mother with young children. Murtain has served as an advisor, provided constructive criticism, and supported the business.

Claudette achieved several outstanding Avon accomplishments including: reaching the Presidents Council level (personal sales exceeding $100,000), achieving Circle of Excellence district sales manager and Senior Executive Unit Leader. Her goal is to unwrap the greatness inside an aspiring leader. The training and skills Claudette has provided for her team showcase her excellence as a mentor. Her business objective is to practice P.A.T.D. (prospect, appoint, train and develop). Claudette continues to participate in community job fairs promoting Avon leadership. Her passion is to help make your dreams come true.

Our Climb to the Top

BY PETE AND GERRY COLBATH

I was born in 1937 in North Conway, New Hampshire. When I was a boy of age three, my parents divorced. For the following three years, I was passed from relative to relative and never knew when or with whom I would live next.

My mother remarried when I was six and I moved in with her and her new husband. I did not realize then that we were poor. We did not have much, however we always had food and clothing. I always worked some kind of job to buy my school clothes. I also needed the money to purchase ski equipment, as I was an avid skier—the first in my school to earn a high school letter as a freshman, and mine was in skiing.

Gerry's life was a lot simpler. She was born in 1938 in Blackshear, Georgia, a small town about 270 miles from Atlanta. She had great, loving parents and was a typical '50s teenage girl. She was the middle of three girls and daddy's pet. While in school, Gerry held a couple of different jobs before becoming a local telephone operator.

Two Lives Merge as One

At seventeen, I joined the Navy. In 1957, I was stationed at Cecil Field in Jacksonville, Florida. Gerry had transferred to Jacksonville after high school and lived with her aunt and two cousins.

That summer, Gerry and I both happened to be at the beach. She picked me up on the beach and chased me until we had a date. During our first date, Gerry proposed to me. On August 2, 1957, her father married us.

We later had a son, Rory Colbath, and a daughter, Tammy Walley. We now have four grandchildren: Gary, Kristin—who will have given us our first great-grandchild by the time you read this—and last but not least, Lance and Linzee.

I was in aviation for ten years and then trained in Explosive Ordinance Disposal. My job was to disarm bombs that may be hazardous to people or property. I went to the top of the enlisted ranks and became an officer. Gerry sold Avon® a couple of times during those years. I retired in 1974 and our family moved to Gerry's hometown of Blackshear, Georgia.

The Fork in the Road

After retiring, I did not want to work for anyone else. Therefore, we tried our hand at several different businesses. No matter what it was, we worked together.

We built a large building on the lot next to our home and started a ceramics business. We held classes and fired the ceramic pieces in the kilns. Unfortunately, the supply companies priced us out of the market.

We already had all the equipment on hand, so we started making pottery to sell. We fired 1000 pieces of pottery each day. I would sell and deliver them to buyers all over the southeast.

In 1985, Gerry and I both had severe cases of lead poisoning caused by the lead-based paints we used to make the pottery. We were in and out of the hospital for about six months for treatments.

In 1987, our son and I started an ostrich ranch and had more than 600 ostriches. While Rory and I cared for the ostriches, Gerry started selling Avon again.

Avon Leads to a Great Life

Gerry was helping the district sales manager start people in their Avon business. Then, she started recruiting for herself for the five percent earning. In 1992, when John Fleming, Avon's former Vice President of U.S. Sales Strategies and Training, started Avon's Leadership program, Gerry converted her recruits to leadership. Soon she made Unit Leader and then Advanced Unit Leader.

I began to see the money potential in the leadership program and got involved. Gerry and I attended the beauty adviser class and became certified appointment makers. We are a team and do most appointments together.

We signed up our son, Rory, and his wife, Angel, in 1996 and they climbed the ladder quickly. They made President's Club in five campaigns and Unit Leader in six. They made Executive Unit Leader (EUL) in 18 months.

Overcoming Life's Challenges

In 1998, Gerry's mother fell and broke her hip. Her daddy needed help, so she moved in with them to help out. Her mother passed away in May of 1999. She stayed with her daddy until he passed away in October of 2000. Had she been working a nine-to-five job, Gerry would have either lost her job or not been able to stay full-time with her parents. This may have slowed her down, yet she met all her obligations. We still received our leadership checks every two weeks.

Things were moving along well, and then on August 13, 2001, we arrived in New Orleans for the National Convention. On the way to our hotel, a pizza delivery truck tried to beat the traffic light, ran into the passenger side of our car, and pushed us across three lanes of traffic into a parking lot.

We spent that week at the trauma center instead of the convention. Gerry had seven broken ribs, a punctured lung, and a broken collarbone. Fortunately, I was uninjured. Avon management came and visited with us and brought goodies from the convention, plus a good luck doll.

After several months of therapy for the broken collarbone, Gerry's shoulder was frozen. Doctors had to break her collarbone again and pin it. Then, she had to return to therapy three times a week—a 120 mile round trip each time. All that time, Gerry had her right arm in a sling and was only able to move her fingers.

Meanwhile our daughter, Tammy, was to be our next EUL and only needed one more Unit Leader to qualify. Instead, however, she gave birth to our third grandchild, Lance—a welcome surprise ten years after his big sister, Kristin. Tammy chose to give up her Avon business.

We had to back up and regroup. At that time, Avon required seniors to have two EULs. We felt like we were on top of the world until about 2008. We had more than 450 representatives in our downline when things started to change. With the rise in gas prices and the increasing cost to advertise in the area, our business expenses grew too high. We averaged over 50,000 miles per year to do appointments and train, therefore we stopped purchasing ads and only prospected in a 100-mile radius from home. Our team decreased from 450 down to 118 representatives by 2010.

Stepping Up to Success

We lost our EUL titles and remained AULs until 2011. Gerry wanted to go to Hawaii, so we started working harder with the people in our downline by taking them out prospecting for recruits. It worked great. Our unit started to grow at a steady pace—with a lot of help from our downline and a big helping hand from Avon's new bonus structure, the best and biggest bonus incentive ever.

We have a tool that truly helps us show how big the money really can be. I teach each new representative that Avon has three ways to earn:

1. Sell the products

2. Build a team under you and make a percentage of their sales

3. Use incentives and receive a monetary bonus. This is money in your mailbox starting with your first recruit. For each qualified recruit, you will receive a bonus check.

Improving Ourselves with Avon

When Gerry first became an Avon representative, she was very quiet. She could sit by you and never speak unless you spoke to her first. Now she will talk to anyone, anywhere, anytime—if it is about Avon.

When Gerry decides to do something, she goes all out. With Avon, she wanted to go to the top in sales. She made President's Club 25 out of her 26 years. She has made Honor Society 23 years and she has made Rose Circle once.

When Gerry decided to go into leadership, her goal from the very start was to achieve Senior Executive Unit Leader (SEUL). Leadership has allowed us to broaden our skills. We have to work with all levels of personnel and train each representative according to their unique personality. This requires us to be adaptable.

As we build our team, we endure the inevitable ups and downs. While the downs can be painful, the ups make you feel like a king. There is so much joy in watching a new representative listen and trust what you are teaching her as she moves up the ladder.

In back-to-back campaigns, two of our brand new representatives made Unit Leader. When one of them went prospecting with us during her second campaign, she gathered names and phone numbers as she gave out books. She managed to acquire 44 names. The next day, she signed up two representatives. She called everyone else on her list and obtained 22 orders, including a $750 order from those prospects. The other new representative made Unit Leader the following campaign. They both earned the $725 bonus.

Share the Success

It is true that there is no magic wand you can wave to make a great team. Here are some tried and true strategies that lead to success:

- **Learn** from other leadership representatives.
- **Use the tools** and events Avon provides for your continued growth.
- **Always do your very best** with what you have and work with those who want to work with you. Take them by the hand and show them the right way, not the fast way.

The leadership role is by far the most challenging part of Avon, yet the most rewarding. You work mostly with young ladies who look to you for their role in Avon. How you handle that role is directly proportional to their success.

Building a team is like starting a fire. You start with small sticks and build a strong fire. Once it is strong enough, you add more wood until you have a bigger, stronger fire. As the fire grows, it generates its own oxygen, which allows it to continue growing. Leadership is the same way. If you build a strong team, it becomes strong enough to make its members' dreams come true.

The Power of Advertising

Anyone who knows Gerry and me will tell you we strongly believe in advertising. A business with no sign is a sign of no business! Here are some effective ways to advertise your business:

- **Wear a name tag.** Gerry never leaves home without wearing hers. We provide name tags for all of our Unit Leaders.
- **Use your vehicles as moving billboards.** Our large motor home has Avon all over it! Our cars are completely wrapped with signs

and Avon products. You can place magnetic signs on your car door. Use mini magnetic product signs to showcase Avon's Bug Guard, Skin So Soft oil, or lipstick.

- **Make your yard into ad space.** Display Avon signs in your yard for people passing by to notice.

Avon has preached "HIP TIME" (taking your new recruit out and showing them how to prospect for customers and recruits). It remains the most successful method of teaching new representatives how to build a customer base. Take them to a mall parking lot or to a storefront. Better yet, go door-to-door.

People no longer want to go door to-door. However, the strategy remains powerful. Our son, Rory, and his wife, Angel, got divorced and Rory kept the Avon team. In 2013, Angel called him and signed up again under him. She was familiar with the "old school" techniques and went door to door. Angel started with 200 books and needed to replenish her supply two days later. She had used the strategy that helped them move up the ladder so quickly when they worked together the first time.

We live in a rural area, which forces us to work harder to find customers. We stop our motor home in any parking lot that will allow us to do so—we always gain permission first. Avon advertising is displayed all over our vehicle and we carry a large stock of Avon products at all times. This brings customers to the motor home, which gives us a chance to offer them the Avon opportunity.

One of the best days we ever had was in a small town in southeast Georgia. We were there to conduct a recruitment training for someone in our downline. She signed up seven representatives that day, all of whom immediately paid their start-up fee of $10.00, and this allowed her to qualify for Unit Leader.

In 2009, Gerry, Rory and I drove to the Avon Leadership Convention in Las Vegas. As usual, our van was completely wrapped with Avon advertising. Along the way, in Alabama, we were stopped at a roadblock. A big road grader approached from behind to pass us. We noticed that it stopped and the driver climbed down from the cab. He walked straight to our van. We wondered what we had done wrong. I rolled the window down to hear what he had to say. "Tell me this is my lucky day," he said. When I asked him why, he replied, "Do you have any of that bug stuff for mosquitoes?" Of course we did, and we sold him two cans. He climbed back up into his grader and drove off. Always promote yourself!

We have been lucky. By attending as many events as we can, we now have Avon friends all over the country. They are like a support team. We always talk with one another and learn from each other. We use that information to pass on to our team.

We have training meetings every Monday evening. The first hour is for all new representatives and the second hour is for all leadership. We find that most new leadership representatives need a lot of training on doing appointments, the proper way to write up a contract, how to build a customer base, and most importantly, how to teach their downline to do these things. We enjoy sharing our knowledge and experience with them to help them achieve their goals.

To Your Success!

We hope our story gives you useful ideas to grow your business. Always work with your team members who want to better themselves. Set goals and revise those goals as you grow. Make use of Avon's excellent, free tools—all you have to do is go to your web page to connect with your upline and district sales manager. Use them! They want you to grow just as much as you do. Use every means available to achieve your goals. Consider pairing sales and leadership. Leadership brings the joy and rewards of training young women how to stand on their own feet and accomplish more than they dreamed possible. Follow your dreams and dream big!

PETE AND GERRY COLBATH

Avon® Senior Executive Unit Leaders

(912) 281-6330
gerrycolbath@hotmail.com
www.youravon.com/gcolbath

Gerry was born in Georgia and Pete was born in New Hampshire. They married in 1957 while Pete was serving in the Navy. They live in the small town of Blackshear, Georgia. Gerry and Pete laid their entrepreneurial foundation by running businesses ranging from ceramics to ostriches. They have traveled, camped, snow skied and water skied, and bowled in men's and women's leagues.

Gerry taught high school for four years. Her Avon journey began after she and Pete suffered lead poisoning from paint on the pottery in their ceramics shop. They later took on square dancing, line dancing and round dancing. They taught country and western dancing, line dancing and Texas Two-Step classes. Their love of dance extended to exhibition dancing at different events including the Georgia State Square Dancing Convention.

Pete and Gerry's Avon business has allowed them to travel all over the United States several times, covering 43 of the lower 48 states. Gerry has never missed an Avon order. They believe that if you want it badly enough, you can achieve anything you set your mind to. They encourage others to think big and dream bigger.

A Journey to Success

I was born in the small town of St Raphael, Haiti. I came to the United States at the age of nine with my brother Harry and my mother to join my father who was already here. I did not speak a word of English and my primary languages are Creole and French. My mother worked in a factory and started selling Avon® to supplement her income when I was in junior high school.

My mother told us she worked in a factory so that we would not have to. Our role, like most children, was to go to school and do well. Unfortunately, my father went back to Haiti and stated that he expected my mother to fall flat on her face. The man of the house managed everything in those days, as was the case with my mother. I started working in my pediatrician's office on my 16th birthday and Harry started the year after. Our earnings helped us purchase clothing, shoes, school supplies and bus fare. It was a relief not having to ask my mother, as she had her hands full with my youngest brother, Dudley, paying for the private school he attended until he graduated from high school.

I attended nursing school because I like to help people, and I worked around my class schedule to pay for tuition. I became a registered nurse, certified in obstetrics. I enjoyed helping to bring babies into the world. My mother always told me that I was always trying to help people, even as a child.

My husband, Larry, and I have been married since 1990. We have two grown children, Kobie and Ayanna. My family plays an active role in my business. They have enjoyed the benefits of my business, like the great family vacations we have taken.

Although it was difficult, I was able to attend most of my children's school functions when they were young. Fortunately, I had some flexibility in my position as a perinatal system coordinator, managing the computer system for our obstetrical team. It was important to me to play an active role with my children, despite working full-time in the hospital and part-time in a clinic. My time was even tighter because I was also a consultant for another direct selling company.

Getting Started with Avon

In the summer of 1998, my mother was diagnosed with end-stage renal failure and passed three months later. A repeated Rose Circle Member, she had sold Avon until the very end. After her passing, we tried to liquidate most of the stock of products she had acquired during nearly thirty years as a representative.

Through the years my mother sold Avon, I had helped with picking up boxes, unpacking, sorting, bagging, writing receipts and delivering orders. I attended special celebrations and never once thought to become an Avon representative. I had my own business for over ten years. Avon was my mother's thing, not mine.

After three months, still grieving over the great loss of my mother, I faced a new dilemma. I had to find a representative in order to purchase the products that I had been using for nearly thirty years. I called my mother's manager to ask about signing up.

The Path to President's Club

When I joined Avon, I discovered I would not have access to the toll-free number I used when helping my mother solve problems. The number was a privilege for President's Club members and I did not want to wait a whole year to reach that level. The cost of long-distance calls could rack up serious charges, no longer an issue with today's cell phone plans. This motivation brought me to the first path on my journey to success—President's Club.

What was I going to do? I set my goals and did the math. I had five campaigns to sell $9,000—that is a lot of Avon. I made President's Club and have been a member every year. Yes, I received my toll-free number. I averaged Rose Circle since my second year with Avon. I even reached McConnell Club one year. The rewards were great, however I told my previous district sales manager I would not do that again, as it was too much work. Rose Circle became my comfort zone.

Stepping Outside My Comfort Zone

A special guest speaker, Evertrue Bell, inspired me at a leadership rally. We were asked to write down our goals for the close of the year and give them to our district sales manager. I was with my downline and had to lead by example. Therefore, I reluctantly wrote my goals and gave them to my manager. I wrote these five goals:

- Number One in Sales Increase
- Number One in Recruiting
- Executive Unit Leader
- Number One in Sales
- McConnell Club

I struggled with the last goal, McConnell Club. I had wished for it deep down, yet felt it was too much work. A gentleman in our district had always been number one and I yearned to beat him just once. At the close of the year, not only did I reach McConnell Club, I also became number one in sales and hit President's Council for the first time. By the President's Club tribute, I had accomplished four out of my five goals. I earned trips to Cancun, Nashville, Las Vegas, Bahamas, Punta Cana, San Diego, Alaska and Hawaii. There is power in writing down a goal; it becomes real. As my journey to success continued, I embraced the second path—leadership.

The Path to Leadership

The sales aspect of Avon always came easily to me. Though I did not really understand leadership, I entered it early in my Avon career. There was money to be made, yet I was going nowhere.

I wanted to know more about leadership and wanted it to work for me. I started asking questions. I went online and called customer service, which referred me to my district sales manager, who referred me to my upline, the person who brought me into Avon.

Fortunately, Avon introduced a leadership certification program consisting of six weekly night classes. There, I met my current division sales manager, who was the trainer. I became a certified appointment maker and could sign people up. I lost my first four recruits quickly, as I had no clue what I was doing.

I re-entered the leadership program in 2003. I was the only one from my district who attended my first leadership seminar in Atlantic City, where top leadership representatives presented. Seeing and hearing them in person made their stories seem more believable. I considered myself only a leadership representative, a candidate. I could not see beyond that.

Then, my former division sales manager said, "You will be an Advance Unit Leader the next time I see you." I gave her a blank look. I was just a leadership representative with a couple of recruits. I brought back to my district ideas like the concepts of the power of three.

Finding Inspiration

The next big event I attended was an Avon product expo at Madison Square Garden in New York. A top seller won the yellow Volkswagen® bug. The video announcing the Woman of Enterprise winner Silvia Tamayo made a lasting impression on me. It was the first time I had heard her story. I thought, *Wow, if she can do that without speaking English, so can I.* I left the event with her story in my head. I was on a mission. I talked to everyone about the Avon opportunity. Before long, I became a Unit Leader and a year later, an Advance Unit Leader.

I said goodbye to my part-time job and the other direct selling company. I wanted to focus on my Avon business, especially on leadership. I became an Executive Unit Leader, completing all five goals I had written down earlier that year.

In 2007, I became a Senior Executive Unit Leader (SEUL). The news came during a conference in Georgia. Once more, no one else from my area attended, however I did not feel as alone as I had when I attended my first leadership seminar. I was among many top performers and my tablemates were exceptional. We networked and got to know each other.

"When we give cheerfully and accept gratefully, everyone is blessed."
—**Maya Angelou, American Poet and Author**

As top performers, we open many doors and change many lives. I look for people like me or even the next Vondell McKenzie, the first leadership representative. I listen to others—their words are clues and may lead me to my next prospect. Most of all, I do not prejudge. The paths on my journey helped me discover the nature of this business. I take my role seriously and believe the compensation I receive is for the success of my downline. The two paths I encountered—President's Club and leadership—needed to come together to achieve my success.

As an SEUL and top seller, I have the tools, knowledge and experience to lead my team to reach their optimal goals. At the International Women's Day and United Nations Summit, I met and spent time with a top leader from the very first seminar I attended. I shared with her how her story inspired me.

At the 2007 National Leadership Conference in Dallas, I was a panelist and presented with three top leaders. Working and presenting with them was a dream come true. Winning an incentive made it possible for three people in my downline to also attend the conference. I am able to share with my team the experience of working and presenting with top representatives. This makes their stories more realistic than just an image on a video.

I remind my team that we, too, have success stories within our unit. I encourage my downline to share how Avon has affected their lives. We feel inspired when someone stands up and says, "You see that big truck outside in the parking lot? My Avon money pays for it and the insurance too," and "My Avon earnings paid for the addition to my mom's house." The response is breathtaking.

At the 2008 leadership conference, I attended my first SEUL event. As fate would have it, I sat next to Silvia Tamayo, the person who inspired me to find out about leadership. I found the courage to speak to her and let her know that her story inspired me to bring my leadership business to where it is today. I met and spent time with my dear friend Donna Reid-Mitchell who personally autographed her book for me. (See Donna Reid-Mitchell's chapter, *My Avon Legacy*, on page 129) The success stories are a great tool that I use and share with my team. It helps them to realize that it can happen with Avon. It is important to pay it forward. I am realizing my dreams every day as I continue on my journey to success.

"I'd rather have one percent of the efforts of one hundred people, than one hundred percent of my own efforts."
—J. Paul Getty, American industrialist

Succeeding with Tools and Hard Work

Today, Avon's support teams are better prepared to provide and direct us so that we can do the same for our teams and customers. Plenty of resources are available at our fingertips, especially with the Internet. As an E-representative, my customers can shop at my online store. I am always looking for new customers and recruits and teach my team members to do the same.

I wake up early and go online. I am able to see what my team is doing using the Downline Manager tool. I can see who has placed orders and who has shopped at my website. I encourage my team to use forwardable emails. The beauty of this is that I do not have to do anything because the emails with promotions and sales are sent to my customers automatically from Avon as if I sent them. This saves time.

As I built my business, my days were full; therefore I got started early. Before going to work, I spent the first couple of hours delivering orders or meeting with new prospects to sign them up. I spoke with three people a day, always prospecting for customers and new representatives. I kept brochures in my car and my purse because you never know when the opportunity may arise. I wore Avon products, as they can be conversation starters. I also spent a couple of hours in the evenings doing some of the same activities.

In 2008, I reached what I thought was the pinnacle of my Avon career, a President Council member and SEUL. Very few representatives hold this dual role. We met our unit goal of $1 million with sales increase of over $500,000, doubling that of the year before. We continue to be a million dollar business with increases every year over the prior year.

Later that year, my leadership status went from SEUL to Executive Leader, which is an advancement unlike that in Corporate America, where top position holders start at lower positions and remain there for unknown lengths of time. My team and I have worked harder than ever regaining our position and continue to do what it takes to maintain our status.

Our hard work paid off in 2009 when the highest Avon honor was bestowed upon me—Woman of Enterprise. I have been on cloud nine belonging to this elite group. Shortly after I received the award, Avon asked me to share my story with representatives in my home country of Haiti. What an honor! I was there to inspire them, yet it was they who inspired me. They do what we do with so much less of what we take for granted here.

Today, many of our representatives come from Corporate America, are stay-at-home moms, are single parents, are students, or are from different cultures. Some juggle family and work. The Avon opportunity offers job security, benefits and financial security. I am in a position to secure my future income while working much less.

When I learned that my full-time position was being eliminated, I felt a little stunned and worried. However, it did not take long to realize what I had in the Avon opportunity. In January 2013, I left my job and became my own boss, working Avon 100 percent. My time is now my own and it gives me the flexibility to move around and meet with my downline at mutually convenient times, not to mention the extra time that I have for my family.

"To whom much is given much is required."
—Luke 12:48

Avon has empowered women all over the word, including my mother and now me. I am a product of that empowerment. I plan to pass my blessings on to others with similar dreams. The honor of Woman of Enterprise comes with the practice of the five Avon values—trust, respect, belief, humility and integrity. I encourage you to practice using Avon's principles and values, along with its available tools. This puts you on the right track for a most profitable business. May you embark on your own journey to success!

MARIE BENOIT-WILCOX

Avon® Senior Executive Unit Leader
McConnell Club Member
Avon Woman of Enterprise 2009
Equipe Espoir
(800) 584-4619
mpbenoit@att.net
www.youravon.com/mbenoitwilcox

Marie was born in Haiti. She worked as a certified obstetric nurse for 24 years. Intrigued by direct sales, Marie joined Avon in 1999 after her mother represented the company for nearly thirty years. She brought her love for helping and teaching others from her nursing background to her business. Marie is a top seller and recruiter with a top leadership team. Avon has allowed her to take her skills to new levels with mentoring and coaching others to achieve their goals and dreams.

Marie has been featured in many publications, including *Redbook, Wall Street Journal, Forbes.com, Essence Magazine, Beauty Fashions* and many company publications. She was also featured in an Avon infomercial and radio commercial. She has been a speaker and presenter at many company venues.

Marie worked her Avon business part-time while working a full-time job at the hospital until December 2012, when her position was eliminated. Marie continues to build her Avon business, helping her team members to realize their dreams while aspiring to reach one of her dreams—to be her own and only boss!

Photograph by: Big Shots Photo Studio

Take Action to Achieve Your Dreams

BY ANGELA KOKORUDZ

I grew up in a small town called Shoal Lake, Manitoba, in Canada. I lived on a farm with two brothers and two sisters. My mom stayed home with us while my father farmed and, in the winter months, worked away at the mines. I loved my childhood and teenage years—they were the best years of my life.

My father was an alcoholic and passed away when I was in my early twenties. He always taught me to be honest and work hard. I feel these were great lessons that have always stuck with me throughout my adult years. My mother was a hard worker. I cannot imagine how she raised five kids and ran a farm by herself. I admire her very much for that.

After dad passed, my mom was left with all of the responsibilities. In addition to caring for her children and the farm, she also had to handle the finances. She started with Partylite® Gifts. I loved helping her pack up her kit and prepare her catalogs and samples. I decided I too was going to join this company and become a businesswoman.

As time went on, my priorities changed. I wanted to move out west to Alberta where there was more money and adventure. My youngest sister and I each packed up a vehicle and drove off to live the dream life.

I taught preschool and also worked as a nanny for wealthy families in Calgary. I would sit in their house and dream of what it would be like to be married and have children. I imagined having my own nanny, a big house, and so much money that lack of finances would never be an issue. Although I was single, I pretended that was my life.

In the meantime, I became pregnant. So much for my big dream! I was in an untruthful and unfaithful relationship, my savings were gone, and I was left with my new, beautiful son, Yusef. Fortunately, I was still employed and received maternity leave for a year. Being a single mom was exhausting. I tried two new businesses which failed.

Making a Fresh Start

I desperately did not want to go back to work. How would I ever be a single mom and work full-time? I decided to make a fresh start and move to Lethbridge, Alberta. I found a job as a daycare director, which I hated.

Being new to the city, I received a visit from The Welcome Wagon committee. They gave me a basket full of information about local services. Included was an Avon® brochure. I looked through it and called to place an order. It was Gayle Bartha who asked me a simple question, "Have you ever thought about being an Avon lady?" I answered politely, "No thanks."

That night, the thoughts kept going through my head. *What a great way to meet your neighbors* and *Come on it's only $20, you can spare that.* I called Gayle the next day and she arrived at my house within the hour. She went through everything about Avon. I was not really interested in all the information, however I listened to her. Then she brought out the sheet about the leadership program. "Reach Executive Unit Leader title within 26 campaigns and you will receive a $5,000 cash bonus!" That sure caught my eye. I signed up and started my adventure with Avon.

Moving Up in the World

I really wanted to meet new people, therefore I purchased 300 brochures and dropped them off in my neighbors' mailboxes. Just three and a half months into the business, I reached President's Club and Advanced Unit Leader. I was seriously unemployable, hated having a boss and did not want to wake up my son to get to work. Therefore, I took a risk and quit my job to start my Avon career full-time.

Later that year, I earned my first all-expenses-paid trip to Toronto and Barbados. There, I had the opportunity to meet all the other top leaders in Canada. I remember the shock when I was at an event, relaxing at a table with a glass of wine. I had kicked my shoes off when they announced my name to come up to the front. I sat up, searched for my shoes and put them on. I was shaking as I walked all the way up to receive the top award for number one leader in recruiting! I sat down in awe that most of the other leaders there had been with Avon for many years, yet I had been with the company less than one year and had become number one. Imagine what I could do if I really tried.

My dream came true. I was able to work from home and be with my son full-time even as a single mom. I reached the goal that was always in the back of my mind—Executive Unit Leader (EUL)—in 26 campaigns. Record breaking.

I was not satisfied at EUL and wanted more. I loved being recognized and knew that if I put my mind to it, I could do much more. How about going to Senior Executive Unit Leader (SEUL) title? I never dreamed of it until it was suggested to me. Me, at the top of a company after I tried so many other businesses and failed—why not? I called Marcia Cota, head of leadership, who was delighted when I told her my goal.

Marcia supported me and encouraged me to do something drastic with my business. She challenged our team to recruit 100 new team-mates in 100 days. I knew recruiting was my strength and agreed to do it. As a team, we recruited 237 new representatives in 100 days and I became Canada's newest SEUL. How amazing it felt to have reached my goal while also breaking another record by achieving this title in just over two years.

Avon Canada launched a red carpet event and ten of my teammates and I earned this incentive. We all were blessed to fly to Toronto. I was so excited to have so many teammates come with me to an event, three of whom had never flown before. We had an amazing time celebrating each other's accomplishments. I was awarded a diamond tennis bracelet for having team sales over $160,000 in four campaigns, another diamond tennis bracelet with rubies for having the most new title growth in my downline, and an all-expenses-paid trip to Spain for holding my executive title for the previous year.

Then, Jennifer Rae asked me to stay on stage. Kristina Swift, director of sales, said we just got the hot-off-the-press camp 20 results. My team had been sitting in the number two spot in the nation and had been working to move up to number one, therefore I thought she was going to announce that we moved up. Then a picture of a car appeared on the screen and she announced that I earned a free car! My mouth dropped. I must have cried in Kristina's arms for five minutes. They say there was not a dry eye in the room.

To earn a free car, you must hold Senior title twenty out of twenty-six campaigns in a year. I worked hard to achieve that. I dreamed and visualized myself in the new car; for it to become a reality in my first year with Senior title is a real dream come true.

Living the Good Life

Avon has changed my life. I have always wanted to travel and love that I can take trips for free with Avon. I have been able to take my son on memorable holidays at five-star resorts in places all over the world that I never thought I would go. We traveled to Australia for three weeks and stayed in a hotel penthouse. It was amazing. We had doors from the main bedroom go out to the roof of the hotel. The ocean was only a few meters away from the hotel. My mom, Sheila; sister, Lasha; brother-in-law, Trevor; niece, Lacey; son, Yusef, and I went to Disney World® in Orlando for ten days. I went to Mexico with a group of friends and had an amazing girls' trip to Vegas, where we rented a limousine for a winery tour before going to see Celine Dion live. It was a once-in-a-lifetime experience. I also earned all-expenses-paid trips with Avon to Prague, where the scenery is beautiful. We had a dinner in a castle where a mini orchestra played music and servers wore white gloves. I could not experience that kind of elegance on a trip I paid for myself. If I had still been working a regular job, I would not have the holiday time or the extra money to have these amazing experiences.

I love the fact that I can be here for my son. When he isn't feeling well I can be home to comfort him. We can wake up when we like, eat breakfast when we want, and not be rushed to get out the door to work. We can go shopping and not look at price tags.

Thanks to my Avon business, I get to live dreams, like the time I took my son to Disney World and bought him everything he asked for. I did not look at the price tag or have any negative thoughts about not being able to afford what he wanted. I could said yes and pay for it in cash. That gave me an awesome feeling.

Being a top leader in Canada means freedom to me—freedom to be my own boss, work when I want, decide when I want to give myself a raise—freedom of time and money. Avon says, "When women are truly self empowered, they can achieve anything—even exceed their expectations!"

Dreams Have Power

You must have a dream to go far in this business. You must have a *why*. What will move you to do the things you do not feel like doing, or the things you fear? What will push you to get out of your comfy bed to go out and grow your business? Place your *why* where you can see it, where you can visualize it daily. I had the leadership flyer beside my bed and dreamed about what I was going to do with that $5,000 cash bonus! Your dream holds power. I encourage you to share it with others so that they will hold you accountable and cheer you on.

When I made the decision to go for SEUL, I knew I had to tell Marcia. I did not want to disappoint her and I wanted to never fail. If I had not kept my goal in mind and not shared it, I would never be where I am today.

If You Wait for the Right Time, the Time May Never Be Right

I was bankrupt and on welfare when I began to build my business. When I took the risk of quitting my job to do Avon full-time, was it the right time to start a business? Of course it was— if I had not taken that risk and decided it was now or never, I would not be a top leader in Canada. Take the bull by the horns and just do it.

Do Not Think—Just Do!

Success requires stepping outside your comfort zone. Do something drastic with your business! Do something you have never done before. Stretch yourself—make goals that challenge you.

I remember when I was an EL and a trainer came to work with me for the first time. She told me to go and talk to someone in the parking lot about Avon. There was no way I would do that, as it was far too uncomfortable for me. I would rather set up tables where people approach me, instead of trying to approach people myself. My trainer encouraged me to try something different. "You can do it!" she said. Even though I was sweating, shaking and stuttering, I managed to approach the person and talk with her. As a result, I acquired a new customer name and phone number. From that moment on, I knew I could approach people about Avon. I now feel comfortable inviting potential Avon ladies to join my Superstar team. Do not think—just do!

Start Your Day with Something Positive

The world can be a negative place. However, you can make it a positive one. Do something uplifting every morning that puts a smile on your face. It may be saying a prayer, doing an affirmation, drinking a cup of coffee, engaging in exercise, or listening to a motivating song. Doing something that starts your day off right makes positive things happen.

Chase Your Dreams

I broke records as the fastest and youngest leader to reach EL and SEL in Canada. I wanted to be home with my son during his five years before starting school. I chased my dream and made it a reality as fast as I could.

Your dream can come true quickly too. If you sit on your dream and just look at it from a distance, you cannot reach it. You must get up and do all you can and leave nothing behind. Then, when you reach your goal you can stand with pride and I say *I left nothing behind.*

I attended events almost every weekend when I was working toward my goal. Setting up tables worked best for me. I found childcare for four to eight hours and went off to work at a table. I invited every woman who walked past my table to learn more about Avon. Imagine how many ladies you could talk to in a six-hour period during an event—usually more than a hundred. Compare that to the number of hours it would it take you to knock on that many doors, work a parking lot, or walk a street? A long time.

Overcome Your Fear

What holds you back? Do you freeze up asking someone for an order, making an up sell, or recruiting and building leaders? Whatever your fear is, you must get over it. Do not let it hold you back. Keep challenging yourself. Be fearless. Think about how you will overcome it and how you will make it. Do something beyond what you have done before.

Never Give up

You have a dream. You have goals and a plan to get there. Do not ever give up! I wanted to quit many times and if I had, I would not be where I am now. Most people quit just before the seed sprouts. After every trial, there is a positive outcome and lesson learned. You must be determined to let nothing stop you! With persistence and discipline, do what you need to grow your business.

Persevere and Succeed

I encourage you to take time to dream. Decide what you want from your business. You will be so proud of yourself and your team when you begin to reach the little dreams and then the big dream. Build big and build fast. Chase your dreams. Remember to have fun—this is your life and you get to decide what happens in your life story. Anything is possible!

ANGELA KOKORUDZ
Senior Executive Unit Leader

(204) 721-2241
angelakokorudz@hotmail.com
www.interavon.ca/angela.kokorudz

Angela lives in Brandon, Manitoba, Canada with her son, Yusef. Her first career was as an early childhood educator. Angela taught preschool for ten years. After her son was born in 2009, she began looking for a way to work from home.

Angela started her Avon® business in December of 2009 and has grown it into a huge success. She has been featured in The Crossroads, and in Rep Café on the Avon website. Upon winning her free one-year car lease in 2013, Angela was featured in multiple newspapers.

Angela is a busy stay-at-home mother, and when she is not working her business, Angela volunteers at her son's school.

My Avon® Legacy

BY DONNA REID-MITCHELL

I grew up with six siblings on the beautiful island of Jamaica, in the rural parish of Clarendon. After graduating high school, I pursued a career in the beauty industry as a professional hair stylist. I was influenced by the awesome work of my older sister, Marjorie Reid-Sharpe. To this day, she remains one of the most accomplished hairstylists in the Caribbean.

I have always prided myself on being a high achiever and my goal was to establish myself as one of the best hairstylists in Jamaica. I was invited to join Soft Sheen Carson's team of elite technical consultants. I traveled extensively throughout Jamaica and the Caribbean conducting educational sessions with professional hairstylists.

My travel throughout the Islands, interacting with many women and men of diverse ethnicity, age groups, and professional and economic backgrounds, was an experience I truly treasure. I gained skills that help me today to interact with ease with my diverse Avon® family.

As a hairstylist, my family members were often my guinea pigs for new hairstyles and product launches. Today, that still holds true with my Avon career.

I continued working as a hairstylist after getting married and having our first child, Yordan. Five years later, I migrated from Jamaica to New York with our son to join my husband who lived in the United States. Soon, my dreams of having a daughter were realized as we welcomed our beautiful Rhiannon. Our family was now complete!

After being home with Rhiannon for two months, I was so enamored with her that I was in no hurry to put her in day care and get back to working in the salon. I wanted to be home to enjoy my baby and soak up every moment watching her big brother assume his new role. I know you can identify with that if you have spent time with a newborn.

Finding a Great Return on Investment

I sought out business opportunities that would allow me to earn some pocket change. I wanted to work from home without much effort until I was ready to go back to the salon full-time. I signed up with Avon and Mary Kay® on the same day to see what both had to offer. I spent $100 to get started with Mary Kay and $10 to sign up with Avon, and I can emphatically say my Avon investment has proven to be my best investment option ever. The return has been so much more than I could have imagined.

I was so excited when I received my Avon start-up kit. I started shopping immediately for all my family's personal care needs—for myself, my son, my mom and my sisters. I can honestly say that my first two campaigns were not very profitable, as most of the orders were mine. I realized quickly that for my Avon business to be profitable, my commission had to exceed what I was ordering to fill my personal needs. I intended to continue to fill all my family's personal care needs from my Avon store.

I am proud to say I acquire all our personal care needs from my Avon store to this day. It is okay to get high on your Avon supply! By wearing my Avon jewelry and apparel, and using the skin care products and cosmetics; I built a customer base quickly because I could speak passionately of my experience with our diverse product offering.

I was making enough money to fulfill my early goal of earning some pocket change until I went back to work full-time in the salon. Plus, I was having a lot of fun expanding my jewelry and cosmetic collection. What more could a girl ask for?

Discovering I Could Make a Difference

Shortly after coming on board, I attended my first district meeting. I thoroughly enjoyed the camaraderie and partnership between the district manager, leadership representatives, and general represent-ative body. This was something I wanted to be a part of. I was intrigued by the stories shared in the room and by the video presentation of the Rich and Famous DVD. That very night, I made a list of potential business partners. I was ready to start changing lives.

I learned that night that Avon was much more than lipsticks and roll-ons. It was a real career opportunity with real income. It was about changing lives one lipstick at a time.

My first recruit was one of my clients from the salon. I signed her up the very next day and that gave me the confidence I needed to offer the opportunity to others. I truly wanted to become a titled leader within four weeks.

Bringing Avon Along with Life Changes

Shortly after I began recruiting, my life changed again. My marriage ended and I became a single mother with two young children. My son, Yordan, who was seven at the time, encouraged me to do more with my Avon business. He told me with conviction, "Mom, you are the best Avon lady I know." Out of the mouths of babes. He even offered to help me grow my business.

That was truly the turning point in changing how I saw my business. It was no longer a hobby. It was now going to become the vehicle of opportunity that would provide financial stability and, ultimately, financial independence for my family and me.

I met with my district manager, Maria Riveria, and created a detailed business plan. I began working daily to achieve my new dreams and goals.

Soaring to a Better Life

My children continue to be my motivation for doing more with my business. Instead of using them as excuses not to excel, they are the reason I constantly work to grow my business. I strategize and brainstorm with them on business-building ideas and ways to support our team. My children are actively involved, as they know this is our business. They are the wind beneath my wings!

I did not own a car when I started my Avon business. One year later, I had saved $6,000 from my part-time Avon business and walked into a Honda dealership in New York and made a deposit on a new SUV. That was my first major purchase and it was financed entirely by my business. We cruised around town that evening totally savoring the moment. That gave me added momentum to accelerate my plans to grow my business and become our main income earner. Then I would have the finances, freedom and flexibility for which I yearned.

My uplines, Bernadette Calamaras, Maria Rivera and Juan Cabrera, really partnered with me as I embarked on building my leadership business. I encourage you to seek coaching from the network marketing professionals at your disposal so that you, too, can benefit from expert coaching and mentoring.

Within 18 months of working my business part time, my Avon earnings exceeded what I was making in the salon full time. I was nervous and hesitant to walk away from a 15-year career, yet I was excited about the possibilities my new career presented. I took a leap of faith and decided to grow wings as I flew.

I finally had the opportunity to be there full time for my children. I never had to miss another baseball game for my son, as I could now afford to have Saturdays off!

My days now revolved around my children. I took Yordan to school in the mornings and brought Rhia—my secret weapon—with me as I went prospecting and to make deliveries. At the end of the afternoons, I picked my son up from school, fixed dinner, helped with homework, and had family time. In the evenings, I devoted more time to following up on leads and generating new business from home. Life was much better now that my career was centered around my family—and it was productive, profitable and fun.

Our next big goal was to move from our one-bedroom apartment in New York into a spacious home. Just three years after being with Avon, that dream became a reality. My family and I were excited and celebrated that accomplishment. If you work consistently at achieving your dreams, they will come true.

With Success Comes Gratitude

I have had an amazing career with Avon and am truly grateful for the positive partnership, coaching and mentoring I have received along the way. I have forged friendships that I might not have made had I not become a part of the Avon Family.

My greatest satisfaction has been seeing the amazing, life-changing results in my downline members. Seeing how Avon has enhanced their lives motivates me to go out daily and look for new business partners to share this life-enhancing opportunity.

I started Avon to be home with my baby, and I have been able to do that. In the last two years, my daughter experienced medical complications and had to be hospitalized several times. I was there with her every second. I have not had to miss out on any of her ongoing appointments or therapy. We have been able to afford the best medical care for her here and outside of the United States, thanks to the business I started for $10. It is wonderful being your own boss! I never have to get permission to do the things I want to.

I had a very sobering moment in March 2013 while attending the Senior Executive Unit Leader (SEUL) Summit in Las Vegas. Vondel McKenzie, SEUL with Avon, spoke and shared with us that she often reflects and wonders what her life would be without Avon. That made me stop and reflect on my own life, pre and post Avon.

I went from being a single mother in a one-bedroom apartment in New York, to being an empowered author, Woman of Enterprise, coach, mentor, professional speaker, successful entrepreneur and, above all, a mother who can take care of all my children's spiritual, financial and emotional needs, without asking permission from a boss to do so.

Because I am my own boss, I have been able to be at the hospital with my daughter if she is sick, while still earning money. The network marketing industry truly is an equal earning opportunity. If I can build a successful multi-million dollar business from home, so can you!

A Vision to Pass a Legacy On

I now have a business I can pass on to my children knowing it has the potential to provide a viable income for them and their families. I encourage you today to grow your sales and leadership business into a legacy that you can transfer to your children. In August 2014, my son will be 18 years old and we are both counting down the days until he can accompany me to Avon events.

Your Avon business can be a valuable legacy for generations to come. Take the time to research what you need to do legally to protect your business. Start by being sure you have a co-applicant. Have a board meeting with your family and educate them about your business. Share where your business is presently and your vision for it in the future at its full potential.

I encourage you to invite and involve your family in all your events and trainings. You can set family business goals, create a dream board together and celebrate milestones, while continuing to set new goals. Be passionate and positive about your business. Seeing how much you love what you do encourages family members to invest their time and energy. Your enthusiasm can be contagious. Success is nothing without sharing it with the ones you love.

Success Strategies

Have clear, well-defined goals. What exactly will success from your Avon business mean to you? Is it money to help you with the household bills, your car note, a family vacation, a full-time income? Be specific. How much time will you invest daily and weekly to make your goals and dreams a reality? Remember, you will be rewarded for your efforts.

Be accountable to yourself. Behave as if you had a boss holding you accountable. You are your own boss and that comes with some responsibility. Set expectations for yourself.

Utilize a daily planner. This keeps you focused and productive. Choose the medium that works best for you—an electronic planner or a paper one—and stick with it.

Have a ninety-day business plan. Evertrue Bell, network marketing professional, helped me realize that all serious network marketers work their business in ninety-day increments. Have a weekly plan of action filled with activities that will be income-generating activities.

Help your team members identify their goals and dreams. Assist them in expanding their dreams and encourage them to think big. Too often, we shrink our dreams to match our budgets, limiting our thoughts to our current financial situation. Now is the right time to expand your dreams and implement a new business plan to match your ambitions.

Incentivize yourself. What will you treat yourself to when you achieve your next business milestone? Consider rewarding yourself with a spa day or dinner with your family at a five-star restaurant. Perhaps you would enjoy a weekend getaway to your dream city, or new jewelry. Maybe even take a trip to another continent. The possibilities are endless.

You can achieve any or all of this by making use of all of the ten streams of income from your Avon business.

1. Brochure sales

2. Internet sales

3. Fundraising

4. Recruiting

5. Developing others

6. Advancing your title

7. Leadership performance bonus

8. Leads and nested representatives in your downline

9. 2% SEUL override

10. Car (Executive bonus)

You deserve to be rewarded for your efforts at the highest level!

Be humble, grateful and gracious. Success is a team effort. Without my hardworking team and partners, none of this would have been possible. I appreciate the positive partnerships I enjoy with my management partners, sister representatives, and downline members. I am grateful that Avon has put us together because our relationships are life changing.

I am truly excited as I think of what we will continue to accomplish. We are enhancing lives one lipstick and one bubble bath at a time. We have just begun to scratch the surface of our possibilities!

Now that I have shared my strategies for success with you, I encourage you to discover those which work best for you. Define your goals and create your ninety-day plan. Reward yourself for milestones and make your own dreams come true as you help others do the same.

DONNA REID-MITCHELL

Avon® Senior Executive Unit Leader
Woman of Enterprise
Mother, Author, International Speaker
Change your dreams, change your life
(866) 467-6417
liveavon5@gmail.com
www.cydcyl.com

After migrating from Jamaica to the United State, Donna settled in New York. While working as an accomplished hairstylist, she joined Avon and established a family owned business that she shares with her two children, Yordan and Rhiannon.

Motivated by the desire for more time with family and the flexibility to engage more in her spiritual activities, Donna has turned her Avon career into a huge success. She enjoys the partnership with her Avon family, spending quality time with her family, engaging in theocratic activities with them, and never having to miss out on any of the activities of her fast growing children. Donna has been blessed with an amazing team of business partners and gets great satisfaction in seeing them grow to be empowered, confident, and successful entrepreneurs.

Donna has been featured in *Essence, Upscale, Networking Times,* and *Empowered Women Magazine.* She is the author of the book *Accelerated Success,* in which she outlines her 7-step Accelerated Business Development Plan.

Your Past Does Not Make Your Future

If I can achieve it, so can you!

BY JO ANN POTTS

This chapter is dedicated to my grandma-ma, Fannie Green, who went to heaven October 20, 2013, just before publishing.

I grew up poor and lived on a farm in the country in Ohio. We worked hard as children, pulling weeds, canning and feeding the animals. Our home was not the greatest. My siblings and I wore yard sale clothes. Every now and then, my mom would use her JCPenney® card and we would get a new outfit. We had fun times and happy times. However, if the walls could talk, they would not talk about the good times, I am sure.

Our stepfather, God rest his soul, was mentally, physically and sexually abusive. He told me I could never do this or that. I could never be any good. I could never have anything. My mother, God rest her soul, told me she was sorry she never really loved me like a mother should love her daughter.

No Silver Spoon Here

I am thankful for my childhood, as it helped me become the fighter that I am. I practiced and practiced my clarinet. I became the best in marching band and the first chair in concert band. However, no matter how well I did, I received no pats on the back, *good job,* or high fives—except the love from my grandma-ma. She did give us the high fives and told us, "I am so proud of you, sweetie."

I remember memorizing the entire 1 Corinthians chapter 13. I was the only Missionette for Jesus to do so and I recited it in front of the entire church. For that, my mom did say, "That's nice."

As a kid, I wanted to go to college, become an accountant for a major company, make millions of dollars, and have a mansion. However, I only received a basic education and never went to college. My dreams and goals took a different path.

As crazy as it sounds, I chose to get pregnant at age 16 so that I could get married and move out on my own. This would get me away from what I was growing up with. I started selling Avon® my senior year in high school.

The first bloody nose I ever had was from my first husband, while pregnant with our second child. Not the happily ever after I had imagined. Four years later, with two daughters in tow, I got a divorce. I quit selling Avon—even though I made President's Club each year. I took on a "real" job, as I knew my ex-husband was not going to support his daughters.

*"Sometimes we get so addicted to murmuring about the past
and blaming the past for everything that we miss our whole future.
You're not going to enjoy your future, and you're not going
to enjoy your right now, if all you can do is be guilty,
ashamed and afraid of your past."*
—**Joyce Meyer, American Christian author and speaker**

Moving On to a Better Life

In 1990, I remarried. We had a son together. My daughters grew up and became mothers themselves—I have eight grandchildren. One day, my husband and I were walking through the Fairfield County Fair Art Hall. I stopped by the Avon booth to enter a drawing. My husband said that I should sell Avon and get the items I use at a discount. His comment encouraged the lady at the booth, who did not stop the discussion until I had signed back up.

This was October 1993. It took the leadership representative until March 1994 to convince me to go back to Avon. I remember saying I would only return if my territory from the 80's was available. It was, and I signed back up.

I sold enough to purchase the products I wanted and I was happy. I was not interested in selling at President's Club level and wanted to keep it simple. As long as I could pay for my Avon fix each campaign—I loved Avon and had been using the products since seventh grade—I was happy.

I was a manager for Chi-Chi's Restaurant, owned a second hand store, and sold Avon on the side. Life was great.

I gave my life back to God in 1998. I began to really hate my restaurant job. I dreaded being around some of my coworkers. I would pull into the parking lot and sit in my car praying I did not have to go in to work. I asked God to help me find a job that I would love and be happy doing.

At my second hand store, I displayed Avon deodorants, Skin So Soft and Clearskin products, along with Avon books, on a small shelf. In one week, I had three people wanting to sign up to sell Avon. I took the first name, then the second. Finally after the third, I thought I should call my manager before I lost the names. After giving her the names, I asked how the leadership program works. I asked if those three names counted toward the required five. The answer was yes. I became a Unit Leader and began to think that maybe Avon could be my "job."

I was blessed to see Lisa Wilbur speak when she came to Columbus, Ohio. What a story she had! It was a rags-to-riches story I could relate to. Like me, she knew what it was like to struggle, to not have much, to scrape enough money together to keep the lights on. If she could do it, so could I. I decided to be the first Lisa Wilbur of Central Ohio—no, all of Ohio!

> *"Better to have a big goal and reach half of it*
> *than to have no goal and reach all of it."*
> **—Joyce Meyer, American Christian author and speaker**

Be Your Own Mentor

I did not have anyone cheering me on, showing me what to do or not to do. Sure, I worked my business, yet not to its full potential. My husband would never let me quit my job at the restaurant, as we needed that paycheck. I worked myself down to one day a week. My leadership checks were nothing to brag about as a Unit Leader.

I started attending every meeting I could. My manager gave me old books and labels and I put books out everywhere I could. I went from being a nobody in my district to being a somebody.

For my district I was:
- Number one for sales increase
- Number two in sales volume
- Best new performer
- Customer Excellence award recipient
- Silver Leadership award recipient
- Rose Circle member—sold over $45,000

For my division I was:
- Number four for customers served
- Number two for sales increase

This was not bad for simply going out there and finding customers. I was proud of myself. I called my mom and took all my awards to show her. Can you guess what she said? "That's nice!" I packed everything up and went to see my grandma-ma. Can you guess what she said? "Wow, honey, I am so proud of you. You got all this? Wow, you really got a lot of stuff. I am so proud of you."

"Somebody needs what you have to give. It may not be your money;
it may be your time. It may be your listening ear. It may be
your arms to encourage. It may be your smile to uplift. Who knows?
Maybe just like that little baby, putting your arm around somebody
and letting him or her know that you care can help begin to heal
that person's heart. Maybe you can give a rescuing hug."
—Joel Osteen, American lay preacher, televangelist
and author

Keep Looking for Opportunities

In 2000, my friend Cookie Woodside and I decided to take advantage of an offering Avon had called Other Venues. We opened a little Avon store and business continued to grow.

I still did not understand the concept of the leadership program. I wish I had someone hitting me upside the head! I had not struggled for team sales because I had built up my customer base. I always sold what my team sales should be. My manager, Kathy Miller, kept cheering me on.

> *"What you receive is directly connected to what you believe."*
> **—Joel Osteen, American lay preacher, televangelist and author**

After three years, my friend left the store. In 2007, I moved my Avon store to a strip center and business began to get even better. God opened every door that needed opening and life was good.

I made the second level of the pay plan, Advanced Unit Leader, then the third level, Executive Unit Leader. Everything was going great and I was on my way to Senior Executive Unit Leader.

> *"Excellence—Take what you have and do the BEST with it."*
> **—Joyce Meyer, American Christian author and speaker**

When Life Gives You Lemons, Make Lemonade

In February 2010, I was asked to care for five of my grandchildren "for a short while." It was best to keep the kids together. I agreed to take them for a short while. Those few months became another few months, and so on. After 11 years, I decided to close my Avon store. I needed more time for my grandchildren.

Life continued to give me lemons. Busy with appointments and visits with the grandchildren, I was not able keep everything going with my Avon business. Two different managers came and went and I lost my Executive Unit Leader status. I felt like a failure. In my mind, I could hear my mom and stepfather saying, *See, I told you so.*

My soon-to-be Executive Unit Leader was thinking of quitting. Life was not good and I wondered if I should quit Avon and find a regular job. I thought about how much better things would be if I had a real job making "real money!"

> *"When you are tempted to give up, your breakthrough is probably just around the corner."*
> —**Joyce Meyer, American Christian author and speaker**

Dig Deep and Find Your Inner Strength

I kept plugging away with Avon, as failure was not an option. In December 2010, my husband and I were given legal custody of two of my granddaughters. This would be long term. I needed to get my Avon business moving to support these children.

In September 2011, we were given legal custody of the girls' three brothers. At the same time, my daughter had another baby, ironically named Serenity. I could not take on another child—a baby.

I spent the first two months of Serenity's life driving back and forth every other day to visit her at the hospital. This left little time for anything else. My husband kept telling me, "Jo, you need to stop. You are going to get too attached. You cannot take on a baby. You cannot do this." His words kicked the fighter in me. I could not let the baby grow up by herself when I had her five siblings.

There was not much happiness in our home. If you tell me I cannot do something, I will show you I can. In March 2012, we received legal custody of Serenity. All six of the children could remain together. Serenity has become Grandpa-pa's girl.

I continued to work the business. Twelve years later, I made it to the top of the pay plan—Senior Executive Unit Leader.

"When you are committed to doing what's right,
you are sowing seeds for God's blessings. You will never go wrong by
taking the high road and doing more than is required."
—Joel Osteen, American lay preacher, televangelist and author

Flexibility, Freedom and Choices

I could not have raised my grandchildren if I had worked a regular job. Day care would be too expensive. A boss would never allow me to come and go as necessary. I am my boss, therefore, I can!

On November 9, 2012, my husband's birthday, we signed papers on a larger home. We are now in a 2200 square-foot home on three acres versus the 1200 square-foot home in the city we were living in. My earnings with Avon and dedication to my business allowed us to do this.

Stay True to Yourself

God is always good and faithful. I think he gets a kick out of putting too much on my plate and watching me try to eat it. God has put many wonderful people in my life through my Avon business. Many have lifted me up when I needed it, and I have done the same for them. I am blessed.

Yes, I had a rough life. However, I choose to not let that become my destiny. I choose to always strive to be the best that I can be.

> *"Don't just accept whatever comes your way in life.*
> *You were born to win; you were born for greatness; you were*
> *created to be a champion in life."*
> **—Joel Osteen, American lay preacher, televangelist and author**

We all have daily choices to make. My past could have led me to prison, blaming others for what I became or did. Instead, I chose to be the best person I can be and to make a difference in other people's lives. What better company to be a part of than Avon, to make this happen?

My hope is that instead of feeling sorry for me, you identify with something in my story and realize that you, too, can have it all.

Work your Avon business as a business and you will have business income. Work your Avon business as a hobby and you will have hobby income.

Remember my dreams and goals as a child? While I never attended college, I am an accountant for a major company—my Avon company, of which I am the CEO! I am on my way to making millions of dollars and millions of friends, and you cannot put a price on that. When my time is up here on Earth, I will have a mansion.

I encourage you to find your inner strength when life throws you challenges. Stay true to yourself and seek the opportunities that will lead you to the life you want to live. Help others get what they want and you will be blessed with what you want. If I can do it, so can you!

JO ANN POTTS

Avon® Senior Executive Unit Leader
The Potts of Gold TEAM
With God ALL things are possible
(740) 652-2866
joannavon@juno.com
www.youravon.com/jpotts
www.start.youravon.com, code: jpotts

Jo Ann first sold Avon as a high school student. She returned in 1994, and six years later, Jo Ann went from a nobody to a somebody in her district with sales over $45,000. From that moment on, Avon was in her blood.

Jo Ann is thankful for the opportunities Avon has given her. She has been repeatedly recognized as a top recruiter and seller and has earned all-expense-paid trips. She has been a member of the Rose Circle, the David H. McConnell Club, and President's Council. Jo Ann encourages her Potts of Gold TEAM by saying that the sky is the limit with Avon and if she can do it, so can they.

Jo Ann's Potts of Gold TEAM is well known in her area of Central Ohio. They can be seen at events shaking their gold pom-poms. Jo Ann recognizes that without her team behind her, she has nothing. Because of them, she has an award winning, million-dollar business. While it has not been an easy journey making it to the top, Jo Ann says it is worth it and encourages her team to get there quicker and make it bigger.

Believe in Your Dreams

BY KAREN TUCKER

My parents taught me the meaning of perseverance. At age 48, my dad became totally disabled, paralyzed from the waist down. Miraculously, he taught himself how to walk again.

My mother put her life on hold to care for him through multiple hospital stays. She selflessly did what was necessary to attend to him and her children.

When I was three months old, doctors diagnosed me with a congenital heart defect. Children's Hospital became my second home. My lips were blue from lack of oxygen, yet I ran around the house with the curiosity of any child. My mother could barely restrain me from playing outside. I did not want to miss out on the adventures of the outdoors.

Early on, doctors told my parents that if I did not have surgery to correct the problem, I would be unable to walk by age 15. I underwent major heart surgery at age 8. Today, I see a cardiologist twice a year to monitor my condition.

School was a struggle for me. At that time, they did not classify children with ADHD (Attention Deficit Hyperactivity Disorder). Instead, I was considered a bad kid. In retrospect, I had ADHD and was slightly dyslexic. This was difficult for my parents because I was the oldest of five siblings. All my siblings received master's degrees and are successful. I was not the smartest child academically, yet I allowed nothing to stop me from pursuing my dreams. Who would have known that I would be the most determined?

I married at 19 and had my first child, Bruce Jr., at 20. Four years later, I gave birth to my daughter, Tiffany. My husband, Bruce, and I have been happily married since 1977.

I worked as a payroll clerk for Jefferson Parish School System. In the summer of 1985, I injured my back and was put on total disability. I could no longer sit or stand for long periods. That was tough for a go-getter. What could I do?

Ding Dong, Avon® Calling

In 1989, my Avon story began. I signed up for Avon and enrolled in a junior college the same day. These were things I could do despite my back disability. I earned an associate's degree and graduated magna cum laude.

At first, I was happy getting a discount on the products I used. Every so often, I would receive a few orders. My district sales manager invited me to a sales meeting where I heard about the wonderful things other Avon representatives were doing. I thought, *if those ladies can do that, so can I.*

I learned about the leadership opportunity and knew the program was for me. I envisioned myself working my Avon business around my children's schedules.

As my children grew, they witnessed me posting my goals on the walls throughout the house. I worked hard to achieve the many incentives Avon offered, and I succeeded. I believe the example I showed them while reaching for my dreams helped foster my children into the adults they are today.

My back problem has improved over the years and Avon offered me the flexibility I needed to grow my business. That reason alone made the Avon business appealing to me.

My district sales manager, Tania Burgess, tells people that there were very few incentives I did not win. She often told me, "If anyone can achieve them, you can."

In spite of 15 surgeries throughout my Avon career, I have never missed sending in an order. You could say my middle name is Perseverance.

> *"The pessimist complains about the wind. The optimist expects*
> *it to change. The leader will adjust the sails."*
> **—John Maxwell, American evangelical Christian author,**
> **speaker and pastor**

I love when people ask me, "Do you still sell Avon?" I always reply that I will do Avon until I am laid to rest. Even after surgery and throughout recovery my subconscious is out recruiting. I bleed Avon!

> *"If you don't fight for what you want, don't cry for what you lost."*
> **—Art Jonak, American writer, editor, speaker and coach**

In 1998, Avon offered an incentive for a trip to Hawaii and I was determined to go. To increase my sales, I used four to ten helpers who acquired sales for me. Within two campaigns, I booked ten fundraisers. I won the trip and achieved President's Council—ten times in thirteen years.

In 2000, I entered an Avon rally as an Advance Unit Leader. My divisional manager, Craig, asked me if I would achieve Senior that year. I had no plan and could not sleep that night. The following morning, I asked my two top unit leaders, Angel and Kim, if they were ready to become Executive Unit Leaders.

Within four weeks, we accomplished our goal and made Avon history! Their efforts allowed my dream of becoming a Senior Executive Unit Leader (SEUL) a reality.

Together, my team placed fifth in Avon's Southeast region. Avon contacted me to speak to top management at the company. They sent me to Canada to discuss the leadership program.

Plan Your Success

To reach the top with Avon, think about these key questions:
- What are your dreams worth?
- Does your team have the sales volume to advance in the Avon leadership program?
- What goals will you act on to realize your dreams?
- What is special about your leadership skills that attract people to your team? What is so special about you that I would want to join your team?
- Will you be available to your team members and go the extra mile to help them succeed?
- What do you envision for your future?

If you chose leadership, put an action plan together for you and your team, and work together every day to achieve your dreams. It does not happen just by wishful thinking or by clicking your heels together three times. It requires dedication and boots on the ground. Work as a well-oiled machine and keep your team moving forward. Only then will you see your team reach its potential. Believe in yourself and in your team. Dare to dream big!

Expect setbacks, hurdles and roadblocks. Adversity builds character and gives your life balance. No one said it would be easy. At different points, I lost four executives and one senior.

Rebuild and Move Forward

Things were going great in July 2005. My team had 725 representatives. We were on fire. Our sales volume was at $3,000,000 yearly. However, the following month, Hurricane Katrina hit and changed that. In a flash, my downline went below 300 representatives. In my hotel room, I watched in horror as the events unfolded in southeast Louisiana. I was devastated—half of my representatives had lost everything they owned.

People could not return home for weeks. When I did return, what I saw was heartbreaking. I immediately knew what had to be done. I had to repair the extensive damage to my house and stay strong.

I noticed there were only a few stores open. I saw this as an opportunity to rebuild my Avon business. I knew God had a plan for me to lead by example, so others would follow. We set up tables on the side of the road and sold $2,500 every two days that we went out. At the end of the year, I had a $100,000 increase in personal sales and earned Avon's Woman of Enterprise Award for 2006.

Hurricane Katrina took its toll. Every time a hurricane comes, we have a setback for a few months. Though challenging at times, God brings you through the bad times.

Mastering My Mindset

In 2010, I became a Certified Dream Coach®. This taught me:

- You must first believe in who you are and get a clear vision of what you are seeking in life.
- Give it your all to make it happen.
- Do not second-guess yourself with doubts.
- Do not settle for what you have. Follow your heart and if you have a longing for something you want, go for it with everything inside you.
- Be persistent—it pays off in the end.
- Believe in your dreams, keep your focus on your goals, and move forward no matter what life throws your way. Only then will you see your dreams flourish no matter what obstacles life hurls at you.

People will need you or you may become ill. In 2012, I severely injured my back for the second time. I needed surgery to place screws in my back and was out of commission for ten months. At the same time, my father became gravely ill and became bed ridden. I had to take my turn as a sitter until my mother felt she could do it by herself.

My family needed me now. I had little time or energy to work my Avon business. Fortunately, I had built a strong Avon team. The benefits of my hard work were paying off. My leadership checks continued to roll in. What a godsend! Thank God I am my own boss and could be there for my parents in their time of need. You, too, can build a strong team to be there when your family needs you.

Self-Employment

Being self-employed means you must be willing to put in the hours necessary to build your business to the point of benefiting from the big bucks. Sometimes you may need to work at least sixty hours in a week. The more time you put into your business, the faster you will achieve the goals that make your dreams come true.

Succeeding may require that you step out of your comfort zone and try new things. That could mean hosting your own team meetings, learning how to text, setting up a conference call, or making a YouTube video.

To be among the top producers, reinvest at least thirty percent of what you earn. Dress for success! Do you have the eye of the tiger? Are you hungry enough to do whatever is needed for your teams to reach their full potential?

If you tell yourself you cannot afford to invest in your business, chances are your business will crumble, along with your income. Get hungry! Make your dreams happen.

Watch your daily reports. Build strong relationships with your leaders. Love them for who they are. Encourage them at every step on their way up the ladder so they will envision the big picture available to them as a team member. Ask, *Where do you see yourself in business in five years?*

The key to success is to stay focused. No matter what you experience, march ahead like a soldier in battle. Never look back. Throughout the New Testament, the apostle Paul told the saints to forge ahead for their reward.

Recognize it is no longer about you. It is about your team and others they bring into the business. As Paul was willing to be of service to the saints, you must be willing to serve your team when needed. Build your team deep. The trophy is worth the fight it took to get where you want to be.

There are great advantages to being your own boss. If you build your team deep, the future leadership checks are your reward. Avon offers this opportunity to anyone willing to dream big, work hard, and envision the grand prize of their dreams come true.

Know your *why*. What is your purpose? Why are you here? What will make you want to work your business every day? Sometimes you will want to quit. You will be tested. The saying can be true; it is lonely at the top. Some may become jealous of your success, yet I encourage you to continue to move ahead and do not fall into their trap. Be a bigger person and love them anyway.

Plant the Seeds of Leadership

Always plant the seeds of leadership to those representatives you feel have leadership potential. I enjoy mentoring my new leaders. I like the excitement in their voice. I am thrilled when my unit leaders succeed. I feel joy as they mature. Leadership is about sharing the same opportunity afforded to you and mentoring others who dare to dream.

Lessons Learned Along the Way

I have learned many lessons as a leadership representative.

Seek team members who are willing to be coached. Help them achieve their dreams and goals, and as a result, they help you achieve yours. Instead of depending on only one person or executive to maintain your title, I recommend you nurture other motivated individuals as well.

In 2013, my Executive Unit Leader lost her title. This put my title at risk. Then, she was short of sales by $300. SEUL cannot earn the Hawaii trip if they are at risk thirty days prior to the trip. Instead of giving up, I pulled out all my tricks. I set up special incentives for her team, which proceeded to achieve its goal of $17,500 in sales. My persistence was rewarded. She got her title back as an executive.

Along with my assistants, Wanda Ramirez and Vivian Cotton, we called the representatives who had not made orders and encouraged more orders. This is vital. Every campaign, your representatives should at least order their brochures even if they do not have an order. Otherwise, their Avon store is closed for two weeks. I earned the trip to Hawaii and it was fantastic!

Fostering Dreams

My passion is to help you dream. If you have forgotten how, I am giving you permission to dream again. If you do not believe in your dreams, who will? I want to be of service to my team. I know this is what God planned for me.

I love the difference it can make for that special representative who gets so excited and shows her appreciation by achieving the goals set up at every level. Like a child learning to walk, from baby steps, she is ready to take one giant leap in fulfilling her dream.

Avon has given me many opportunities. It allowed me to travel the world and broaden my horizons. I love the freedom of being my own boss. It allows me to dream bigger.

Tools of the Trade

Persistence. Studies indicate that all successful people have persistence. They are willing to take the time necessary to accomplish their task and to persevere in the face of difficult odds. Persistence means never giving up. Fight the good fight. Stay focused. Rise above the circumstances of life. If you are determined, believe in yourself. Be willing to pay the price and take action. The possibilities are endless!

Today Avon representatives have many success tools at their disposal. Listen to the weekly free calls, or the playbacks, from the comfort of your home to keep your focus. While driving, listen to motivational CD's of Les Brown and all the dreams-madereal.com calls, that are stories from Avon representatives. What is holding you back from achieving your dreams?

Avon is about making your dreams come true by building relationships with other team members. Today, my team is over 550 representatives and we continue to build. You, too, can make your dreams come true.

Overcome the challenges that come your way, take advantages of the tools of the trade, and follow your dreams!

KAREN TUCKER

Avon® Senior Executive Unit Leader
Certified Dream Coach® and Group Leader
It's all about believing in your dreams!
(504) 628-5176, 1-855-685-2866
www.karenbtucker.com
www.youravon.com/ktucker
www.facebook.com/avonkarentucker

Karen lives in the small town of Belle Chasse, Louisiana, outside of New Orleans. She has been a stay-at-home, entrepreneurial mom for thirty years. She knows how to get what she wants through persistence. Even after overcoming tragedy, Karen is a living example of never giving up.

After Hurricane Katrina, she bounced back by having a $100,000 Increase Personal Sales in her direct sales business and earned Avon's Woman of Enterprise Award 2006. She has earned numerous awards for Personal Sales, number one recruiter, and the number one Leadership Group Sales in her division for 24 years. Karen has won trips throughout the country and has spoken at many national conventions. Her success has been featured in many publications and company articles, including *Networking Times* and the *Plaquemines Gazette*.

Karen is a Certified Dream Coach and Dream Coach Group Leader through Dream University and she loves helping others achieve their dreams through coaching. Karen is also an inspiring speaker and workshop presenter. Her passion is to give others hope to dream again so that they can make their dreams come true and earn the money their families need.

Changing a Hobby into a Million Dollar Business

BY LISA SCOLA

"Success and happiness are not matters of chance but choice."
**—Zig Ziglar, American author, salesman
and motivational speaker**

I grew up an only child in Austintown, Ohio. I found that not having siblings was a challenge, yet it built character. When I was young, every opportunity was available to me. I was not spoiled, however I definitely did not want for much. I started ice skating at six years old and thought that maybe it would be a career I would embrace.

When I was fifteen years old, my parents divorced and my father left my mother and me. It was devastating and we were left to figure out how to live on our own. All my plans changed overnight. I started working at McDonalds® and my mom, who did everything she could to sustain my lifestyle, was behind me with every decision I ever made. Our bond grew stronger than ever.

When I was 18, I sold Avon® for a short time. I wish now that someone would have showed me the opportunities.

When I graduated from high school, I decided to go to a business college in Pittsburgh. I figured that in less than a year, I could move away to somewhere warmer and get a good job. However, I abandoned that goal for a relationship instead and returned home to Ohio. That was a huge game-changer for what my life would have been like.

I worked several office jobs and always made enough money to pay my bills and maintain my finances. My primary focus was to get married and have children. It took me longer than I had planned, but at age 25 I married the man I came home to and started my life. I was blessed with an opportunity to teach ice skating at a local ice rink and had a nice job at a steel foundry. My husband was self-employed and we had a pretty good life. We traveled and spent a lot of time remodeling our home.

All the while, we worked on starting a family. However, not everything in my life came easily. It took us three years to have my first son, Zackary. When he was born, my mom was diagnosed with chronic obstructive pulmonary disease, a lung disease. After going on maternity leave, I was laid off—a blessing in disguise.

Choosing to Stay at Home

I always dreamed of being a stay-at-home mom. I did not like the idea of going to work and not seeing my children grow up. The decision not to look for work was difficult and I sacrificed a lot by staying home. However, it was worth every moment. It allowed me to share time with my son and my mom.

When Zack turned one, I learned I was pregnant with our second child. Almost six months into that pregnancy, I lost the baby, a boy. This was an extremely difficult time in my life. However, it led me toward finding my relationship with God again.

Amazingly, the same month I would have been due to deliver the baby, I discovered I was pregnant again. If that was not my God taking care of me, I do not know what was! Mikayla, my angel from God was born in June.

Having two little ones to care for was the best thing I could imagine. Staying home with them was wonderful. However, I struggled with bills my husband did not feel it was necessary to pay and with credit that was just getting awful. Still, I did not regret my decision to stay home and knew somehow things would work out.

When Mikayla turned one, I wanted to do something other than watch cartoons. I started thinking about finishing college, however that would put me into more debt with no promise of a good paying job. I considered part-time work, yet realized the money I would make would go to pay a babysitter and that would not be worth it.

Starting My Avon Journey

One morning, the answer came to me: *That's it—I'll do direct sales!* The question was, which one? I narrowed it down rather quickly. I refused to do parties, especially at night. I certainly did not want to put a ton of money into a business when I had no idea if it would work or not. Avon was a possibility that came up time and time again. I remembered a friend of ours who sold Avon and decided to give her a call and find out how I could start up. Within a week, my manager, Anita, came over and had me up and running. It cost me $15 and I obtained plenty of books and training materials to get me started.

For the first few years, I did not do a lot of selling. I participated in all the trainings and passed out books to friends and family. However, there was no serious need to try making it a profitable business right away. I did, however, see that Avon had a lot to offer. I knew that if I worked it right, the business would grow with my children. Therefore, I decided that I would put more time and energy into my Avon business as my kids grew.

Discovering Leadership

Two years into my journey, a good friend inquired about selling Avon. I knew the company offered a leadership program and thought this might be a good opportunity for me to start doing a bit more with this hobby I loved so much. I met with her manager and signed her up that week. This was a life-changing day for me. With my management and secretarial skills, I was off and running.

I had access to information online and could learn from Avon's *Rich and Famous* and *Dreams* magazines, however there were no leaders in my area. Therefore, I mentored with top leadership outside my area. I attended every event possible in an effort to learn how to get to the top of the Avon pay scale.

I could hardly wait to become a Senior Executive Unit Leader (SEUL). It took me two years to become an Advanced Unit Leader and not much longer after that to achieve Executive Unit Leader (EUL). My business more than doubled in sales and I went from selling at President's Club level all the way to Rose Circle—and I did this with two little kids by my side all day and with my mom sitting next to me. It was truly a family business.

I made good use of all the remarkable training Avon offers. I took advantage of the beauty training and even became a Certified Beauty

Advisor Trainer, one of my goals! I saw a great future with Avon. I worked to build the best possible team, SEUL was right around the corner, and I could not wait to achieve my goal for myself, my kids and my family.

Just when I thought everything was going perfectly, I found out I was pregnant with our third child. I was shocked and a bit set back. My marriage was having some problems and I had a hard time seeing how a new baby was going to fit into my busy schedule.

Holding On Through Life Transitions

Mikayla was five and Zack was seven when John was born. My world really changed when this little guy was born. He truly was an Avon baby; right there with me all the time, while his brother and sister were at school. It was just John and me with my mom, out there finding customers and prospecting for recruits.

I would love to say that life was perfect and we all lived happily ever after. However, that was not the case. My husband had an affair and I decided to move on without him. During this hard time of divorce and heartache, I really had to do a lot of soul searching. My team had been on top but started to dwindle away, my mom's health was getting worse and I felt like I was going to lose everything. Thank God for my supportive manager and close friends.

When God closes a door he always leaves a window open. I met some truly supportive friends at that time. My Avon leadership went all the way back down to Advanced Unit Leader. Thankfully, my customers, who were very supportive of my life changing events, really stuck with me through it all.

I remember my son, Zackary's response when I told him I was going to have to get a job. The concerned look on his face and his words, "Mommy, you won't be here when I get home from school!" sent chills down my spine. I gave him a big hug and told him, "Okay, then I will just make this Avon business do it." And that is exactly what I did.

My mom's health was worsening. Through all of my Avon career, she was always the one person who helped with everything. She was my right hand and cheerleader. Then it dawned on me that there was someone else in my life who encouraged and helped me through everything, and although he was a man, I felt he could make something of his own Avon business. He joined my business and became my cheerleader.

When life comes at me in full force, I have learned to push harder and not let it steam roll me over. I soon moved back up to EUL and could see that my dream for SEUL was getting so close. In the summer of 2010, my divorce of almost four years was finally over. I went to the Avon conference in Las Vegas and set my goal for SEUL by Christmas.

Two days after I returned from Las Vegas, my mom passed away. Sometimes I think life dishes stuff out to you just to see if you will hold onto God's neck and let him pull you through. My mother's death was the hardest thing I have ever had to go through. As an only child, I felt I had no one to turn to. I only had myself and my kids. I needed to be strong for my three kids and not give up on my dreams for my business.

Staying Strong

Avon has changed our lives more than I could ever have dreamed and I can only see it getting better. I made SEUL that Christmas. The feeling I had that morning when I looked at my computer and saw those few little words was very overwhelming.

I know my mom is by my side every day helping me and giving me strength. I have a diverse team and each member has his or her strengths we can pull from. My children have seen me struggle and pull through. They have learned lessons in life that a normal job would never be able to teach them. They brag about their mom all the time and it feels good to be such a positive role model for them.

Avon sends top leaders on trips that I have only dreamed about. I have been blessed enough with my business to be able to take my children on vacations and enjoy living much easier than we ever have.

Success Strategies

Any business you want to embark on brings challenges. Nothing is ever just going to happen. It takes hard work and perseverance. Here are a few strategies I have learned:

- **Be the Avon Lady.** Go out of your way to make sure everyone knows you as the "Avon Lady."
- **Tap the wisdom of others.** Leaders before you have developed tools that may work for you. Early on, I captured a lot of the wonderful marketing techniques that Lisa Wilber had put into place.
- **Live and breathe your business.** Make your business part of your everyday life. Everywhere I go, Avon becomes part of my conversations with people.
- **Lift as you climb.** You have the opportunity to change lives. Enjoy the pleasure of helping others achieve their goals as you achieve yours.
- **Be your own boss.** Work harder for yourself than you would for anyone else. Meet your goals and make your dreams come true. I believe that is what keeps the drive going.

Although the money has been nice, having my business is about more than that. It is also about meeting and sharing with others what I do and helping them do the same. I believe we can give back to the world what God has so freely given us.

We all have hardships we must endure. Stay strong through the challenges and keep your eye on what matters to you. Make use of every resource you can get your hands on and become an expert. Decide what is important for you and focus on what you need to do to make that happen. Success is yours!

LISA SCOLA

Avon® Senior Executive Unit Leader
Mentor, Trainer, Speaker, Author
(866) 892-9544
(330) 792-4538
(330) 518-8761
www.youravon.com/avonlisas
www.start.avon.com, code: avonlisas

Lisa Scola lives in Youngstown, Ohio. She grew up an only child who loved to ice skate. Instilled with an excellent work ethic, Lisa worked various office jobs and taught ice skating.

After starting a family, Lisa's determination to be a stay-at-home mom was the driving force to start her Avon business and build it into a profitable endeavor. Lisa endured a difficult divorce and became a single parent of three children. Her business struggled, yet she persevered and chose to hold on to her Avon business. Lisa rebuilt her business all the way back to the top. She has been selling Avon since 2000.

Lisa has earned President's Club level, or above, every year she has been with Avon. Her team has achieved over $1 million in sales and continues to grow. Lisa has earned many trips through Avon and looks forward to many more. Lisa expresses pride to have chosen Avon as the business that would change her life. Her children support her and love that she is an Avon Lady and realize her career choice has changed their lives.

Time, Dedication and Motivation* Create Success

BY MARIA STREET

I grew up outside Dallas, Texas, in the city of Farmer Branch. I attended a local Catholic school through the eighth grade and then went to high school in Carrollton.

In 1981, I married Peter Street, who grew up in the same area. We attended the same local junior college. Pete went on to a technical school where he obtained his Airframe and Power Plant license. Eventually, we both took positions in major corporations.

In the late 1980's, my company was in the process of restructuring. I was known as the one they could always depend on to stay late or arrive early. I was basically married to my job. During this time, we were also expecting our first child. When my employer merged with another company, I did not have enough seniority to keep my position. I could have taken on a different position, however the pay was lower and the hours fewer.

Our daughter, Courtney, was born and I decided to take unemployment as an option and to stay home with her. I stayed home for several months and we decided it was time for me to go back to work. I found a position in customer service and found a daycare for Courtney. My position did not last long because I received frequent calls to go and pick Courtney up.

We continued to take her to the daycare while I looked for another job. Eventually, I began working at the daycare center so that they would not charge us for Courtney's care. This was also short lived, as the center could not meet my pay requirement and I decided to quit.

Some of the daycare parents wanted to know where I was going. When I told them I would stay home, several parents wanted me to watch their children. I decided to become a licensed, in-home daycare provider until Courtney was school age and then I would go back to the corporate world. However, when our second child, Meghan, was born in November 1993, the plan changed and we decided to keep our daycare open a little longer.

In 1995, when Courtney became school age, I was the mom who wanted to help with school activities. I joined the parent and teacher association and served as the hospitality chair on the board.

The first project was to put on a spaghetti dinner event. I had to find a committee that would work with me to make sure this dinner was a success. I met Cass Lincecum, a lady who was unbelievably organized. She was a stay-at-home mom who sold Avon® in the subdivision next to mine. Not everyone had a computer back then, yet Cass could make anything we needed to hold the spaghetti dinner on the computer—the tickets, charts, posters and check lists.

Together, we asked for donations for everything we needed. We transformed the school cafeteria into an Italian restaurant for the evening. The event was an overwhelming success and we were proud of our accomplishment.

I ran an in-home licensed day care and managed a network marketing product line. Courtney was in school and Meghan was still at home with me, along with the day care children.

A few weeks after we had put on the spaghetti dinner event together, Cass came by to deliver an Avon order I had placed with her. She was on her way to shop for a new van for her husband, Chris. I told her that my network marketing company offered a van tax, title, and license, free for its top performing managers, or a car allowance. I gave an opportunity kit with the company video. I asked her to take a look at it and I would give her a call in the morning. The next morning, she came by the house and told me the opportunity would be too much work.

Diving into Avon

I asked Cass to share her opportunity with me. She brought me ten catalogs and a contract. I completed the Avon contract, distributed the catalogs to my day care moms to take to their offices, and called Cass to ask what to do next. I expressed that I found it hard to believe she made money selling lipstick. I asked her to show me her pay-check stub, which she brought when she delivered more supplies. After reviewing my contract and collecting my $20 start-up fee, Cass shared with me how Avon worked. I could not believe the income she was making.

Once I got started, my day care moms noticed more and more boxes being delivered with each order. Their priority was what was best for their children. They wanted me to have more one-on-one time with their children, which meant keeping my adult-to-child ratio as low as possible. The moms asked how much Avon they would have to sell at the office in order for me to not have to take on additional day care children. That is how I started selling to others—my day care moms took care of the orders and deliveries while I took care of their children. I did not even need to leave the house!

We continued that process for a few years. The moms brought in enough orders to cover mother's days out for all of them. I transported them, picked them up, and used those days to recruit and start my team.

One day, when I was hosting a home party for my other direct selling company, Cass was in attendance. She noticed the presentation booklet I used and it gave her an idea. She developed a similar kind of presentation book for our Avon team. The book featured Ms. Albee, some of our products, and the earnings structure for leadership.

Shortly after Cass created the presentation booklet, Avon came out with a kit to issue to new representatives. Cass held local trainings that were open to everyone. The district sales manager also held meetings. Later that year, I became the district assistant while the manager was out on a medical leave. What I learned as the assistant, and from the meetings I attended, created a solid foundation for my business. Cass then became the first Senior Executive Unit Leader (SEUL) for the Mustang Division. I became the first Executive Unit Leader (EUL) of my district in March 2001.

Working Around Life's Roadblocks

That year, we decided to relocate to Saginaw, Texas, and build a new home. Things were going well and on schedule to move in before school started in the fall. We had just sold our home when we ran into some construction challenges with the new home. It would not be completed before school started. We took a temporary residence in my mother-in-law's home and life became interesting as we commuted the kids back and forth to school. I could not wait to sell and prospect in my new area. It was going be terrific!

Then came another setback. My mother, who was a diabetic, was hospitalized. She was blind, on dialysis, and later became paralyzed on one side. I worked my schedule around her appointments. Every weekend and school break, the kids and I were either at the hospital or the nursing home.

Thank goodness for my Avon business, which allowed me great flexibility while still making the income I needed. If I had worked a regular job, I would have been fired for taking off so much time to be with my mother. I continued to sell Avon products and maintain the team. I am grateful for my wonderful team members who were there for me.

In March of 2003, my mother decided to discontinue her dialysis and passed away a few days later. In the meantime, Cass had been undergoing treatment to fight ovarian cancer. Two months after my mother died, Cass also lost the battle with her disease. They were both strong women whom I admired.

Time to Get Back to Work

To grow a business, you need a solid foundation and visibility in the community. I was still new to Saginaw and needed to meet people to grow my business. I joined the Saginaw Area Chamber of Commerce and became an ambassador and then the ambassador coordinator for a few years.

The ambassadors helped assist with the ribbon cuttings for new businesses in the area, along with a photo opportunity and an introduction of you and your business at each event. I was the Small Business of Year in 2004 and a Leadership Northwest graduate of 2008. I attended all of the luncheons and networking events to build my business. Visibility is key to growth!

The Team Continues to Grow

Once the team started growing again, it was time to build some foundations. I believe you need to have a solid foundation to build a strong team. It may take you longer to grow, however your representatives will be stronger—slow and steady. I started a series of training classes with limited seating. I created a team mission statement to go along with the trainings.

This is my Mission Statement for my downline training sessions: *These sessions were created to start your business with a solid foundation of information needed to have and maintain a successful independent business with a pay structure and schedule that you create for yourself. I will show you and tell you but you will not see the results until you implement them yourself—you are in control. I am here to help those who want to be successful and believe in a business plan for personal success.*

Over the years, I have gathered flyers and information and compiled them into a series of trainings. These trainings have been overwhelmingly successful in taking representatives from non-leadership title to Unit Leader (UL) and from zero sales to several hundred dollars in sales. Here are some examples of topics I cover in my trainings:

• How and where to sell and prospect
• How to look at a previous brochure online

- How to read and project reports
- How to use all mail plans for team growth and a consistent check
- How to conduct an appointment
- How to set up for job and craft fairs
- The A-Z of running a business
- Calendar management

When it comes to your calendar, remember that you are in control of your business. Do not let your business run you. I strongly encourage you to let a calendar work for you. Place in your calendar your personal activities first—those are your rocks. Then, add your order days, delivery days and events. I prefer at-a-glance style calendars. Color code items so that you can just glance and see if you are available on a particular day.

Relationship-Building is Key

Get to know your team members and their families. Know their goals and dreams to help achieve them. Know their favorite colors, flowers and restaurants.

Who would not be thrilled with an extra $100? Reward and celebrate individuals with the things they like. Meet team members for lunch or coffee. If the kids are out of school, meet at the local McDonald's®.

Income Equals Ambition

Avon allows you to build an unlimited income and business on *your* schedule. What you put into your business is what you receive out of your business. Avon is not "get rich quick." There is money to be made, yet some representatives give up before they deposit the money.

It does not happen overnight. My first check with Avon was $7.28; not even enough for them cut the check, which had to be over $10. The next check was enough to take the family to Cici's® Pizza. The next paid the phone bill, then the electric bill, and now my checks pay the mortgage and car loans.

Today, Avon has several incentive plans in place through which you can earn bonuses. You can also earn consistent leadership checks by training your team to sell. Set sales goals and incentives.

Not Everyone Wants to Recruit

About one in every twenty representatives is interested in recruiting. These are the leaders and advancement does take time. I was an EUL for eleven years. Never pre-judge and always ask. You will move to higher levels in leadership when you build a great team of representatives who see this as a business opportunity and who have the necessary motivation and drive. You cannot want it more than they do. Take the team members out and teach them how to prospect. Develop a thirty-second commercial with them. Develop surveys on different products. Teach them how.

Teach How to Sell

Make sure all representatives know how to sell by demonstrating with the front cover of the brochure. Show them the scented pages at the time of appointment so they can share with their new customers. Explain the skin care consultation card for repeat sales. Teach your representatives how to re-invest in demos.

The Rewards

Avon always has incentives to reward you for the work you have done. Know about the different levels of recognition. Track your team's success and encourage them to move forward. Every year, Avon offers a trip under the President's recognition program. The year 2013 was my first year to achieve the trip as an SEUL. We traveled to Hawaii and stayed at the Hilton® Hawaiian Village Waikiki Beach Resort in Honolulu. The celebration was awesome! The event recognized the top performers in personal sales and leadership volume. You can get there with your business.

I hope that I have given you some inspiration and information to help you with your business. Remember that your income is equal to your ambition. Do not give up before you get started. Be visible in your community. Offer quality, consistent service to your customers. Build relationships with your team. Work your business like a business—*you* run the business, do not let the business run you. Things will then fall into place.

MARIA A. STREET
Avon® Senior Executive Unit Leader
Rose Circle Member

(817) 306-8875
mariastreet@sbcglobal.net
www.youravon.com/mstreet
www.start.avon.com, code: mstreet

Maria joined Avon on National Representative's Day in March of 1996. What started as an account for personal use soon became a rewarding career where income is equal to ambition.

Today, Maria is a Senior Executive Unit Leader who trains, mentors and motivates a team of over 400 awesome representatives. This has team sold in excess of $1 million for several years. The team has received numerous awards over the years for Sales Increase, Sales Volume and Recruiting at the District and Division Levels. Maria offers training sessions to help all representatives achieve higher levels in personal sales and recruiting. She holds a graduation celebration once a team member has achieved the criteria. Maria expresses to others that she loves selling a product that is usable and consumable—and also has a 100 percent guarantee.

Since 2001, Maria has resided in Saginaw, Texas, (just north of Fort Worth) with her husband, Peter, and their two daughters, Courtney and Meghan Street. Maria enjoys entertaining and decorating for special occasions, hosting home parties and shopping.

Play Big

to Live Big

BY PAM KNIGHT

When I was a young girl growing up in South Carolina, my mom signed me up for piano lessons. My love of the piano and music became an important part of my young life, and at the age of 11 I began to play for youth functions at our church. A year later, our church pianist had to take a medical leave of absence and I was asked to fill her shoes until she returned. I was good, just not great. However, the personnel committee and my mom convinced me I was perfect for the job.

Other than grueling piano recitals year after year, it was the first time I remember saying goodbye to my comfort zone. I was afraid, yet found the strength to give it my best. As I reflect back, I remind myself that it is okay to try new things while being afraid. If every situation is comfortable, then you are not pushing yourself to grow into a stronger person and reach your maximum potential.

My mom wanted to make sure I played loud enough to be heard. Therefore, prior to every church service, she always said, "Play big." That one bit of advice that I heard many times during my early pianist years has been a driving force throughout my life. I only came to that realization recently when I was telling a friend about my mom's weekly instruction—and it hit me like a brick. I have always attempted to play big throughout my life. Thanks, Jo Ann Taffer, my biggest cheerleader and mom, for pushing me and believing in me, even before I did! I now realize that I have been in training to reach Avon®'s top leadership position since I was 12 years old.

Discovering Network Marketing

In the mid-nineties, a friend sold Jafra® cosmetics and needed one more recruit to reach her team's goal. She asked me to join and I said yes. Although network marketing and direct sales were not terms I truly understood, I loved my new business venture. I was having so much fun, yet had no expectations or goals.

The business was totally different from anything I had ever known. I found myself wanting to learn more and decided to see what I could do with this new "hobby." Little did I know, it was the path that would eventually evolve into my Avon journey.

My Jafra experience lasted for a year. Shortly afterward, I began selling Finesse® Jewelry, a new direct sales company based out of Memphis, Tennessee. I achieved a great deal of success. Within a year with Finesse, I surprisingly built the largest team the company had seen in its early years. Looking back, my success with Finesse was due to my love of the product, excitement for sharing the business with my friends, and enthusiasm about helping them reach their goals. That same concept holds true as I work with my Avon team today.

My Finesse leaders began duplicating exactly what I was doing and we put this young company on the map in the southeast. Surprisingly, leadership came naturally to me. No one in this young company really knew what I needed to do. I mapped my team's growth and plan of action week by week. I am still amazed they followed me and even more amazed we were such a success!

Several years later, Finesse Jewelry merged with Jeunique International® from California. Unfortunately, its diverse line of products was not a good fit and caused my thriving team to disintegrate. I felt sad that our Jeunique futures were dissolving. However, in retrospect, the experience taught me many skills and a tougher resilience to face challenging adventures in my direct sales future.

From Avon Customer to Avon Representative

Fast forward to May of 2005. I loved Avon products and referred to myself as an Avon junkie. Whenever my representative at the time delivered my order and a new brochure, I felt like a kid in a candy store.

I had retired from all my direct sales attempts and had extra time on my hands, even working full-time as an accounting manager for a local heating, ventilation and air conditioning company. I decided to become an Avon representative—to get a discount on the products.

A Great Leader Must Be a Great Seller

I was having fun again and decided to find a few customers. I developed a plan based on Avon's *"Power of 3"* promotion. The Play Big strategy was kicking in once again. To build a solid customer sales base while working full time, I selected two businesses every weekday and asked if I could leave a brochure. I maintained a list which included the business name, phone number and contact person.

When you implement this strategy, you will have collected twenty business prospects per campaign. For the following campaign, repeat the process with the newest brochure, with the same business prospects, and continue to repeat until they have seen four brochures. Treat your new prospects as if they were already your customers.

Your customer base builds over this four-campaign period. Some will buy and some will not. Maintain your new customers and eliminate those who never make a purchase. Continue to repeat this process with a new set of businesses. This is how I built a $30,000 annual sales business on my lunch hour and on my way home from work. Was it fast and easy? No. Was it worth it? Absolutely!

Having a successful sales business is important to growing a successful team. Set the example. It is imperative to make sales or no one makes money. I share this with all my representatives. They do not have to manage it exactly as I did, however the concept of putting the Avon brochures into a potential customer's hands on a consistent basis is the way to establish the sales side of your business.

Tips for Being a Great Seller

- **Be consistent.** Deliver brochures each campaign to potential and established customers.
- **Make it easy to do business with you.** This will knock their socks off!
- **Show appreciation.** Your customers want to feel special and appreciated.
- **Listen to your customers.** Sometimes Avon representatives can be therapists for their customers.
- **Follow up quickly.** They will stay with you forever.
- **Be the best.** Provide the highest quality of service your customers have ever encountered.

- **Tell everyone.** Make sure all your family, friends and business acquaintances know you have your own Avon business.
- **Ask the question.** It is easy to say, "Have you seen an Avon brochure lately?"
- **Show enthusiasm.** Be excited and proud to say, "I want to be your Avon lady."

On to Leadership

I did not participate in Avon's prestigious leadership program for the first few years of my Avon career. I first sold successfully at Avon's Honor Society selling level, $20,000 to $30,000 annually, for four years. People had encouraged me many times to try leadership to maximize my Avon earnings. Then, within a one-week period, two random people asked me for information on becoming an Avon representative. Unfortunately, I had no current information to help them start their Avon business. My district manager had a leadership meeting scheduled and I decided to attend. I wanted to simply get enough information to help the two people. However, what I saw at that meeting inspired me to start building my own Avon team. The timing was perfect and I am so grateful today that these two people needed my help.

I decided that I would create a letter and share my new leadership dream with all of my customers and friends. Nervously, I placed this letter in every customer's order and sent it to everyone in my contact list that I wanted on my team. I was afraid, however I remembered my own philosophy on proceeding despite fear.

At each interval during this period, I found something tangible related to the level I was working to attain. Avon's *Believe in Your Success* brochure, which shows the various titles of achievement along with the qualifications and payouts, stayed with me at all times. I looked at it every day and imagined myself at that title and earning at the next level. The dream was already in my heart and this helped keep it in my head. I knew many people who had achieved different levels of success within leadership and I decided to follow in their footsteps.

From the beginning, I expected success in this area of my business and determined to never stop believing my goal could be achieved. I quickly realized recruiting was actually like selling. Become good at the process and repeat, repeat, repeat.

Stepping Away from the Comfort Zone

The challenge was in place. I realized I needed to be around anyone who was more successful in the business than I was in order to learn their habits and characteristics. I took a friend to lunch who was a marketing expert and asked his advice for a starving Unit Leader. He advised me to make my business and team seem bigger in my mind than it was at that moment. We all want to be part of something great and successful. Therefore, as I shared the opportunity in those early months, I kept my friend's advice in mind and it helped other people want to join my team.

If a high-ranking leadership representative was attending any Avon function close enough for me to attend, I was there! Have sponge-like properties and be receptive to learning from others' successes. I tell my team to find someone successful and be a copycat. I feel honored when others duplicate what has worked for me.

I went from Unit Leader (UL) to Advanced Unit Leader (AUL) to Executive Unit Leader (EUL) and finally, in the spring of 2012, I titled as Senior Executive Unit Leader (SEUL). People frequently ask how I reached the top level of Avon's leadership program quickly and I tell them it is three things—connection, connection, connection.

I resolved from the beginning that anyone on my team would know clearly that they had support from me, their upline. As my team has grown, I have had to tweak how I communicate with each generation. I make sure they know I am just an email or text away. Working with different generations is important for building the depth of a strong and stable team.

We all have the desire to be connected to something big, something great. We have an invisible sign on our heads that says, "Make me feel special." Always acknowledge team member achievements and let everyone know how important they are to your team.

Keys to Success: Repetition and Persistence

I challenge you to work on the goal in your heart. Have something to look at daily to keep it in the forefront of your mind. Become great at selling and recruiting and teach others to do the same. Be the example everyone wants to follow.

The neat thing is that once you become great at recruiting, you do not have to keep "recreating the wheel." Instead, just continue to repeat your process. Yes, you continue tweaking, adapting and improving, however repetition and persistence is the key to growing a successful team of superstars!

Discipline has always been the driving force that led to my success. It determines your destiny. Do not let failure be an option. Know where you are and where you are going. Then, simply fill in the blanks.

I am with the right company at the right time with cutting-edge products I can offer to my customers at a competitive price. I continuously adjust and try new things. I am resolved to reaching my goal of being one of Avon's top earners by working with one customer at a time, one representative at a time, and one leader at a time.

I find pure joy in working with my leaders, teaching them to say the right words, investing time in them, letting them know I believe in them, and expecting them to do well. The belief you have in your team can transfer into a surge of self-confidence and they soon become an important part of your Avon family. One of the most favorite parts of leadership is watching someone's dreams transform to reality. I am seeing lives and futures transformed and my young team has only begun!

Even more important than believing in my team, I believe in a God who created me in His image and my goal is to serve Him daily. He guides and sustains me through great days and rough days. I thank Him daily for salvation, health, a good mind, and family and friends that make my life complete. My favorite Bible verse is;

> *He that dwells in the shelter of the Most High will rest*
> *in the shadow of the Almighty. I will say of the Lord, "He is my refuge*
> *and my fortress, my God, in whom I trust."*
> **—Psalms 91: 1-2**

I hope you have gleaned a bit of excitement to join me in that sometimes uncomfortable yet rewarding place to live—that place just on the other side of your comfort zone. Will you get frustrated, tired and worn down? Will there be days when you want to give up? I promise you will want to quit more times that you could imagine. Just solidly resolve to stay focused on the goal of joining the elite top-earners of Avon.

*"You will never leave where you are until you decide
where you would rather be."*
**—Dexter Yager, American direct sales pioneer
and mentor**

You have the power to achieve the life you were meant to live. When you choose a successful financial future, you can help others by showing them a better way and impact your world by leaving a footprint that shows you live life to the fullest and want to help others achieve their dreams. Dream, plan, prepare, execute and Play Big!

PAM KNIGHT

Avon® Senior Executive Unit Leader

(864) 423-1834
pam711@charter.net
www.youravon.com/pknight

Pam Knight is a proud South Carolinian who grew up in Greenville. Her supportive, traditional family and friends encouraged her to be the best of the best. Pam excelled through her childhood and early adult life, yet was more comfortable away from the limelight. This makes her Avon journey even more amazing.

During her first direct sales venture with Finesse® Jewelry, and even today, Pam has maintained a full-time position as accounting manager for a local HVAC company. She has become an expert in time management as a result of so many important responsibilities and goals.

You can catch Pam on Sundays playing the organ at Welcome Baptist Church and then enjoying special Sunday lunches with her husband, Donnie, and her mom. You cannot mention Pam's son and daughter-in-law, Matt and Caroline, without seeing a big smile pop up on her face. Other special loves in her life include her dad, Kim and Alexander, her dachshunds, Max and Molly, and working out with her awesome trainer, Amanda. Pam realizes how blessed she is and wakes up every day being thankful for life and striving to make the most of every hour of every day.

Achieving the American Dream *

BY ESTHER LUNIS

I cannot really say whether business found me or I found it, however business was always a part of my life. It started with my mom, her sisters and, my favorite of all—my maternal grandma, Alcine. We call "Grann." Even though Grann has crossed over to eternity now, the memories remain.

My first defining moment in life was when my parents announced they would leave my siblings and me in search of a better life. They moved to America, then Grann moved in with us.

Business 101

We ran a sewing shop out of our home. It was always busy with people dropping off and picking up dresses for weddings, Communion and other occasions. Uniform season was the busiest of all. We all played a role, from sweeping to hemming and more.

Customized fabric buttons and buckles were the trend, and Grann ran that part of the business. I would watch her every chance I got and rehearse the process in my mind over and over, waiting for the opportunity to move from my job of sewing class helper to buttons and buckles specialist. As you can see, I was not your typical 11-year-old.

I remember the day vividly. My little fingers could finally wrap the fabric around the metal buckle with such precision. My heart beat faster, both with fear and excitement, and many thoughts flooded my mind. What if I messed up? What will I spend the money on? In spite of all that went on in my mind, my hands were steady, crafting the first of my many masterpieces. Until then, I had only watched and this was my big moment. All the observation had paid off, and since my fingers were smaller than Grann's, I was even faster than she was. After I had completed every detail, I brought the finished product out to the customer. She inspected it and paid me. There, in that moment, I fell in love with business.

I looked forward to one day running things in Grann's absence. Up until then, I had kept all the money I collected. It never occurred to me that it was not mine to keep. It was simple reasoning—I make the buckle, therefore I keep the money! One day, after much deficit and the numbers not adding up, Grann put the puzzle together. In her loving way, she broke it down for my 11-year-old brain to process. She said, "If you keep all the money, how am I going to buy more supplies for the business?" That day, I learned what I thought to be the worst words in the world—cost of goods.

I quickly made peace and submitted to the process. I learned quickly that some money was better than no money. On that day, a partnership was formed. When Grann was not home and I was not in school, I was in charge. That day, I fell in love with leadership.

Sooner than expected, my life changed again. Being the oldest, I was able to come to the United States and live with my parents. It would be an understatement to say that leaving behind my three siblings was bitter sweet. After a long, gruesome process, they all made it to the United States.

As I look back now, I am so grateful that I had the grace to sit and learn from such a great woman. The skills I learned from my grandma were the foundation I would build upon for years to come. What if I had only played in the yard?

America, Land of the Free

America gave an opportunity that nowhere else offered and with hard work and perseverance, my family prospered. In spite of the challenge of learning English as a second language, I was determined to succeed. The French language was so different than English. Watching TV and hearing laughter drove me crazy—I did not understand what they were laughing about. Going to school was even more frustrating.

That first summer, I was determined to learn English and my goal was to be fluent by the next school year. I developed my own rigid reading regimen and my dad took me to the local library several times a week. When September came, I was able to skip two levels of the English as a Second Language program. I got my first job at Bradlees® department store, graduated high school, and attended community college. Time was moving fast.

I cannot say that I was looking for love, however it definitely found me. In 1989, I married the love of my life. I can say it was the best decision I ever made—besides becoming a born again Christian many years before that.

Through the years, I found many ways to earn money. I ran a house cleaning business, a hair accessories business, a babysitting service, a gift basket business and a catering business. I am a firm believer in doing whatever your hands can find to do.

Avon®— What If?

Four years into married life, I gave birth to my beautiful baby girl who weighed seven pounds, eleven ounces. I wondered if I could somehow be a stay-at-home mom. It was the logical choice because I had no family to help me where I lived in New Jersey and a part-time income would all go to pay for day care. The idea of being a full-time mom was foreign in my neighborhood, yet I felt the call.

In 1993, my Avon lady, who lived upstairs from me, announced she was moving to Boston, Massachusetts. After months of being unable to replenish my favorite products, I opened my own account. I was excited about the products, demos and discounts, and fully enjoyed the convenience of buying direct. I made no attempt to earn money, however I was happy with the experience.

One day, after months of small orders or no orders, I received a pleasant call from the district manager, Rose Davidson, who invited me to a sales meeting. She said I had nothing to lose, and I agreed to attend. It was amazing! You could touch and see the products before you ordered them and there were door prizes. To a stay-at-home mom, that was heaven. Then there was a recognitions portion of the meeting during which representatives were acknowledged for top sales. I became quiet, wondering if it was a gimmick. Can people really sell that much at a time? While I did not even have a $100 order yet, some of these ladies where doing $2,000 to $5,000 in sales! I was amazed they could have such large orders.

After the meeting, I was the first one to find the manager and ask her to explain these numbers. She suggested I talk to a couple of the ladies there who accomplished top sales, and I did. Since then, I have networked with so many district and divisional managers and fellow business owners, each bringing their own expertise and wealth of knowledge into the mix.

Some of the strategies I learned that day, and continue to learn, are:
• Network with people who give you access to their friends and family.
• Advertise—get out there and put in the legwork necessary to promote your business with books, business cards and flyers.
• Provide good customer service—do unto others as you would like done unto you.
• Commit to a product every campaign—introduce it and sell it.
• Commit to applying the principles you have learned.

Low and behold, by the next cycle I was a President's Club member. Then, I was in the Honor Society, followed by Rose Circle. I discovered that the $5,000 orders were not a lie! Please keep in mind that I was not driving back then.

Confronting the Fear

Leadership is recruiting and training others to do what you do, and even more successfully. I loved the potential of the leadership program, however my biggest obstacle was the challenge I felt with talking to people. People who know me today find that difficult to believe!

I was terrified of speaking to people. The idea of speaking to perfect strangers paralyzed me from the inside out. To make matters worse,

I inherited an extremely low voice from my mom. We are very soft-spoken women. That can be really cute if you are on a date or if you work for one of those adult phone lines, however for everyday life and business, it is not a benefit.

I had to quickly learn—and I am still learning—how to be heard. I found speaking louder is just plain exhausting, yet with practice, it gets easier. I used to think people ignored me (or they thought I ignored them), however it turns out they simply did not hear me. Although I was afraid, I chose to move forward with the dream of building a successful business.

Over the years, I have experienced many twists and turns, major and minor setbacks. However, I stay on course. One hurdle after another, I have learned to walk the path. I have learned that even when the pace is slow, as long as I keep moving, I am heading somewhere.

From 2000 to 2003, I went from being the parent of one older child, to becoming the parent of three children. "Traumatic" does not even describe that experience. I was no longer waking the path—I was crawling it, yet I was still moving. I never stop moving.

In 2003, I made a conscious decision to focus and do Avon exclusively. As a result, I have been able to get more out of it. Every time I pay a bill or go on a nice, all-expense-paid trip, I feel an awesome sense of personal accomplishment.

Eight Success Strategies that Work

- Know what you want. Once you are in, be all in—double-minded-ness is a curse to success.
- Never stop moving forward.

- Create healthy boundaries. As Polonius says in Hamlet, "To thine own self be true." Choose who qualifies as your inner circle.
- Get in a loop with people who challenge and encourage you in positive ways. Two or three people are more than enough.
- Get involved. Attend meetings, rallies, conferences and more.
- Surround yourself with positive people who love the business enough to acknowledge the bad, yet focus on the good.
- Be around the people whom you aspire to be like.
- Treat everyone with love and respect, even when you do not feel he or she deserves it. I find love to be a long-term investment where the dividend always pay out. Life is too short and the world is very small.

Making Dreams Come True

Recently, I went to visit a representative at her house. As I complimented her on her house, she explained how she was able to have such a lovely home. She reminded me that she received a letter certifying that she was a representative and the bank accepted her extra income from selling Avon in order to qualify for the loan as a single mom.

Another individual, an exceptional leader, started a school in a remote part of Haiti where no schools previously existed. She now educates and feeds more than 400 children and has plans to expand. I have met countless people whose lives, including mine, have been impacted in amazing ways because of their Avon incomes. We have purchased cars or houses. Some have paid for private school tuition, ballet lessons, music lessons or vacations. Many have paid off debts they did not think possible to pay.

My pastor quotes this poem, which I have adopted into my own life:

*"Great it is to dream the dream
when you stand in youth
by the starry stream.
But a greater thing is to fight
life through, and say at the end
the dream is true."*
—Edwin Markham, American poet

With hard work and perseverance, you can make your own dream come true. Observe and learn from the experts and surround yourself with positive people. Ask questions, treat everyone with love and respect, and conquer the fears that hold you back. You, too, can say the dream is true! Live the American dream!

ESTHER LUNIS
Avon® Senior Executive Unit Leader

(973) 699-1380
www.youravon.com/elunis
www.start.avon.com, code: elunis
estherforbeauty@yahoo.com

Esther has been with Avon since 1993 and has been married to Yves Lunis since 1989. Together they have three children: Kwani, Joshua and Jeremiah.

In the 2007-2008 cycle, for the first time, Esther's team sales surpassed the million dollar mark. In 2011, she achieved her long-time goal of Senior Executive Unit Leader (SEUL). Self-employment has afforded Esther the opportunity to raise her children hands-on and to follow her passion for philanthropic work. Esther believes that people and time are the most valuable assets in this world and that they are to be handled with care. Esther's business has afforded her many opportunities to travel, including destinations like Alaska and Hawaii. Her goal is to partner, train and develop leaders throughout the fifty states.

When she is not working her business, Esther can be found at The Love of Jesus Family Church where she oversees a food pantry and homeless ministry outreach that serves more than 300 families each week.

Her basic belief is *Do unto others as you would have them to do to you.* Luke 6:31

Roll Around in the M.U.D. — Master Your Ultimate Desires

Roll up your sleeves and dig deep to find your inner hidden treasures

BY CARRIE PURGASON

Ever since I was a kid growing up in Fort Wayne, Indiana, I had a desire to go to the top. My parents encouraged my brother and me to do our best in everything we did.

I enjoyed dance lessons and playing on a girls baseball team. I participated in musicals and played the flute and piano. In seventh grade, when I did not make the cheerleading squad as a cheerleader, I suited up in a big, furry eagle costume and became the best mascot I could be, continuing to learn the cheers while revving up the crowd. I made the squad as a cheerleader the following year!

In high school, I joined the marching band color guard and learned about leadership as a captain. We went to a regional competition where the fields were muddy and soaked with water. We had a routine that required us to roll around on the ground barefooted in white unitards. In order to advance to finals, we had to put on the best show possible. We had one of our best performances and became finalists.

The next week at state competition, one of our directors gave us all a pin with the acronym MUD in a heart shape—Master Your Ultimate Desires. I keep that memory close to my heart and the message still resonates to this day. In order to move forward, sometimes you really do have to roll around in the dirt a bit—and have fun doing it—to reach your next goal.

I went to Ball State University to become a teacher and ended up instead with a degree in public relations and a minor in marketing. Before starting my student teaching, I had a heart-to-heart talk with my parents. I loved teaching, yet felt a pull to go in a different direction. My leadership experiences in college—sorority chapter president, peer mentor to incoming freshmen, and drum major in the Pride of Mid-America marching band—taught me a lot about myself. I took an extra year, charged ahead, took full-time classes, and worked full-time hours. I often left my apartment at 8:00 a.m. and did not return until after midnight.

I worked at Taco Bell® upon graduation and was promoted to assistant manager—much to the dismay of the seven others vying for the position. I learned to overcome objections and gain their trust.

Although I was ready to go to work in the public relations field, I took the Taco Bell position and stayed in Muncie, Indiana, for the next year. I was in debt and could not afford to move. My electricity and phone were turned off and I could not pay my bills. Therefore, I needed to stay in town, get myself organized, and work on paying off my debts before seeking a job related to my degree.

The next year, I worked as a first-level warehouse manager for Target®, where I met my soon-to-be husband and we quickly hit it off. Our manager crew had a great sense of teamwork and commitment. When the employees were on break, we kept the system going, kept boxes moving, and raised the bar. We became one of the top buildings in the network by rolling up our sleeves and getting the job done, with constant communication between departments and a sense of team unity. I later applied these traits to my Avon® business.

I was a lucky girl to marry my best friend, Adam, and in 2002 we had our first child, Alex. I proudly entered our marriage debt-free. I decided to become a stay-at-home mother and quit the job that I loved.

Starting My Avon Journey

Although my husband conveyed work stories to me, I felt lonely. For the first time, I was not always on the go. I loved my baby boy, yet needed to do something more. When he was about three months old, I found an Avon brochure on my doorstep. This was a sign! I quickly devoured the brochure. I had not seen an Avon brochure since childhood, when our Avon Lady, MaryAnn, came over to share samples and take orders.

I made an appointment, a district manager came to my house, and I signed up. Thus began my new life. I studied the materials, reading every word. I remember the exhilaration of opening my first box when my order arrived. Today, I conjure up that feeling when I sign up a new team member.

Early on, I made a lucky mistake and accidentally ordered 400 brochures instead of 40. Instead of returning them, I made it my mission to hand out each and every one. Alex came along in his stroller and we walked up and down the street passing out books.

A year later, I had about 140 customers in 3 different counties. Keeping up with brochure and order deliveries while building a team and caring for my family was a challenge. I could not always make sure customers had the latest brochure and was falling behind. I started bulk mailing the brochures to save me time to grow my team. I quickly saw the timesavings and increased sales. I started helping some team members do the same and they had similar results. Soon, online Avon friends asked for help and I volunteered. I enjoyed helping others succeed.

By 2004, I had a nice-size team in Indianapolis and had reached Honor Society in sales. I mailed my own brochures and helped others mail theirs through a small Yahoo!® group I had started. Mark® had launched and I loved the brand. I reconnected with college contacts and recruited for Mark on local campuses. Avon asked me to host the first official Mark chat with representatives in another Avon-Mark Yahoo! group I started. Things were moving along wonderfully.

Adam was doing very well at work and was offered a chance to move to Columbus, Ohio, and open a new distribution center there. We decided to take the risk, sell our first home, and move. It was hard to leave my customers and team members behind. We incorporated my "little" mailing business and named the company Consultant Depot. Today, we continue to mail brochures for thousands of representatives across the country each campaign.

I continued to build my team in Columbus. A year later my daughter, Jessica, was born. My kids were with me as I worked my Avon business. They watched me prep and deliver orders, go to appointments and sales meetings, and pass out brochures in parking lots and parks. Now, they help me to do all of those tasks and receive a percentage of the order in return. Sometimes, their canvassing results in a call months later. They are shocked at how a seed planted long ago can flourish after time has passed. I hope they take that entrepreneurial lesson with them as they grow.

The Turning Point

One day, Adam was off work and I decided to join another district manager in prospecting in her area. We spent the day handing out books and talking with businesses. One lady wanted to sign up and we met at her house after she got off work. We went over the materials to help her get started with her business. Afterward, I asked the district manager if she needed me to sign the contract. She had decided to keep the sign-up for herself to meet her numbers. I was dumbstruck. I had taken the whole day away from my babies to help build my business and felt as if it was all a waste. It left a bad taste in my mouth and upset me.

I decided to take a break from leadership. Consultant Depot was growing and I was happy to make a bigger impact in others' lives through helping them distribute their brochures, saving them time and money. We launched a new website, consultantdepot.com, and I spent more time on our mailing business and growing my customer base.

Over the next several years, we moved our family three more times. One of my first generation representatives went on to become an Executive Unit Leader (EUL). I did less recruiting and did not take advantage of the fact that I had such a strong leader on my team.

When we lived in Seattle, Avon was celebrating its 125th anniversary and I attended my first meeting in years. I realized that things had changed. We moved back to Indianapolis in the summer of 2011. My once EUL had moved to Florida and hung up her Avon hat. The remaining twenty members of her team rolled up to me over time.

My daughter was going to first grade and would be in school all day for the first time. I decided to reach out to my new team members, who did not know who I was.

I first called her only surviving Unit Leader, Pamela Boles, a grandmother with a giving heart, who was now in my first generation. We met and connected immediately. She encouraged me to restart building my team.

Invest in Yes

Believe in your Success was a new leadership incentive Avon rolled out to representatives. With my newfound time and rekindled Avon spirit, I decided to check out the new leadership program. I loved the idea of earning different types of bonus money along the way to reaching our goals. I was determined to go to the top.

I started by building my first generation and decided to treat my new team members differently than in the past. At the time of appointment, I gave them:
• The regular getting started kit
• As many samples as they wanted
• Extra order books
• The branded cover and pen set
• A folder with additional information to help them get started on the path to success
• An Avon calendar personalized with their order and delivery dates
• Lots of books—often cases of books if they promised to use them

If it was an online appointment, I sent a box in the mail with the same materials. I *invested* in their success. I *believed* in the company and their ability to make it with this business. I *delighted* in their excitement and watching the possibilities of their dreams becoming a reality.

To be a leader of leaders is one of my ultimate desires. There is something deep within me that always has yearned for this—to help others to be their best. I reached out to my long-time top sellers and educated them about the leadership opportunity. We started by redeveloping their Who Do You Know (WDYK) list and techniques to fit prospecting into their everyday. They had what it took to be great sellers, now I would help them build a team and duplicate their sales success with others.

Pam was ready to dig deep, too. Together we grew our teams and developed new leaders. In the spring of 2012, I was invited to take part in the pilot program of AUL Academy, which changed the course of my leadership destiny. I gained new skills and training that opened my eyes to a whole new way to grow and develop my team. The Direct Selling Women's Alliance provided this training to AUL Academy participants with weekly conference calls, training modules and support.

Achieving Leadership Goals

In 2012, Pam and I both reached our next leadership goals. She became an EUL and I reached Advanced Unit Leader (AUL). This is a very important part of my strategy to reach my goals. You see, by helping others attain their goals, you can reach yours without even realizing how much easier it will become for you. My new Unit Leader, Suzie, Pam and myself, all celebrated by dancing in the parking lot! We could not believe how much fun this was and little did I know that we had only just begun.

Over the next few months, I *rolled around in the mud.* I prospected, recruited, and sold my Avon heart out, enriched by the added training I was receiving in the AUL Academy. Avon introduced additional incentives and with every program, we decided to go for the top. Soon, I had 103 new representatives nested to our team in three generations. This was crucial to my success, though meeting the requirements did not come easy. Hard work does pay off!

Later in 2012, I reached EUL and had four leaders in my first generation. Just three campaigns later, I reached Senior Executive Unit Leader (SEUL) and had six leaders in my first generation, including my EUL, Pam. I graduated and was the Valedictorian of our AUL Academy class in our graduation in Orlando—paid for by Avon—for being the first in the class to reach SEUL. What an honor!

Reaching SEUL was my original goal, however the lessons learned and friendships created along the way are priceless and an unexpected gift from the journey. When my team reached five generations deep, it was a moment to celebrate. Each team member is like family to me. We have helped each other tackle many of life's obstacles, including divorce, domestic violence, substance abuse and debt. However, we are able to rise above and celebrate new births, marriages, children's successes and dreams coming true.

Today, I remain an SEUL and am proud to help others start their own Avon journeys. Consultant Depot continues to bulk mail brochures for representatives in all fifty states.

We moved into our sixth home, outside Richmond, Virginia. It was much more difficult to leave my 300+ team in Indiana this time. I look forward to making connections in Virginia and it is time to up my game even more than ever before. We are launching a new team website, www.investinyes.com, which will help unite our team members near and far with trainings, webinars, team incentives and motivation. I am constantly learning from other leaders who have large teams over multiple states about how to become more successful.

I am fearful that I may lose my SEUL title with this latest move and as a younger team, it has been challenging. Transitioning my kids to their new surroundings is my first priority. However, I have proven before to myself that you can marry together business building and family life. Anything is possible if you put your mind to it and act.

I am thankful for my journey with Avon and Consultant Depot. My family has been blessed with a more enriched lifestyle with my Avon earnings, including purchasing a new car, taking my family to Disney World®, planning a cruise with the kids, and letting them play on travel baseball teams and participate with competitive dance teams. I want the same for you and cannot wait until one of my team members earns a higher check than I do!

Master Your Ultimate Desires

I have learned many successful strategies over the years. I encourage you to try them for yourself:

1. **Constantly expand your knowledge and learn from others.**

2. **Be your team members' biggest cheerleader—celebrate their success!**

3. **Include your family in your Avon business—have fun together!**

4. **Do not give up on your "career" Unit Leaders—or yourself!**

5. **Teach solid money management skills from the start.**

Keep going after your dreams and do not give up. It is okay to take time off for a while and adjust to your family needs at the time. That is the beauty of running your own business! However, saddle up on that horse again and go for it! *Master your ultimate desires!*

CARRIE PURGASON
Avon® Senior Executive Unit Leader

Carrie@consultantdepot.com
1-855-YES-2-AVON
www.consultantdepot.com
www.investinyes.com

Carrie was born and raised in Fort Wayne, Indiana. Today she lives just outside Richmond, Virginia. She graduated from Ball State University in 2000 where she majored in public relations and minored in marketing. Carrie started her Avon business in 2002 and leads her successful, Invest in Yes Team.

Carrie is the founder and owner of Consultant Depot, a direct mail for direct sales resource serving Avon representatives since 2003. She is a member of the Direct Selling Women's Alliance, with which she has earned Elite Certification. She graduated from Avon's AUL Academy in 2012 as Valedictorian. Carrie has volunteered as an advisor for her college sorority, Sigma Kappa. She also volunteers at her kids' schools.

Carrie lives with her husband, Adam, her son, Alex and her daughter, Jessica. In her free time, Carrie enjoys reading, playing piano and cheering on her kids at their sports games and dance competitions.

Success Is a Journey, Not a Destination

BY KENDALL CRONK AND MARIA DELGADO-CRONK

Two Worlds Apart

We came from two vastly different worlds. Maria was born in Matamoros, Mexico, to parents who were Catholic and very proud of their culture and traditions. Her father, with only a second grade education, was a master tailor and owned his own tailor shop from the time he was 21.

At the age of ten, Maria's family immigrated to America for a "better" life. That was what they told her. However, coming to America did not seem better to Maria. You see, while living in Mexico, the family had both a maid and a cook. When they arrived in the United States, Maria became both the maid and cook. To make matters worse, she was dropped into a school where her teachers only spoke a language that was not hers.

I, on the other hand, was born in Santa Barbara, California, to Baptist parents who were very "white." My mother was a homemaker and my father an electrical engineer. When I was eight years old, my family moved to a farm in New Mexico where I lived until I graduated from school.

Growing up on a farm, you learn quickly that cows do not "give" milk; you must "take" every bit of it. Cows require being milked every morning—even before having to get on the bus for a one-hour ride to school, and then they need milking again every night. The routine continues regardless of 110-degree summers, or winters that can get down to 42 degrees below zero. I learned to work at an early age—hard work.

School was not an easy thing for me. Having a learning disability made school more than a challenge. When they kindly "gave" me my diploma, I could only spell at the second grade level.

Becoming One

When Maria and I met in 1989, it was like two worlds colliding. I had never been married and Maria had just ended a marriage of 15 years. We were very set in our own routines. Imagine never having to be responsible for anyone but yourself and then becoming the head of a household of seven. At one time, we had four teenagers all at the same time under one roof. You wondered if everyone would live through it!

Playing the Hand You Are Dealt

Maria and I were both dealt very different hands, yet equally difficult. We could not ask for a reshuffle to try for a new hand.

Growing up, every new teacher I had just knew that he or she would be the one who could fix me. However, they quickly resigned themselves to "Kendall is just different."

Maria on the other hand, at the age of 15, became pregnant and left home and school to get married and have her child. By the time she was 18, when most people her age were graduating from school, Maria was raising three children, running a household, and working full-time.

We both played the hands that life had dealt us. I learned to over compensate for my problems. I discovered ways to hide my problems. I even taught myself how to work around what I lacked. According to the studies, Maria should have ended up in the welfare system and at the bottom of the financial ladder.

> *"You don't have to be great to start,*
> *but you have to start to be great."*
> **—Zig Ziglar, American author, salesman**
> **and motivational speaker**

Knowing Your Seat on the Bus

As partners in business and in life, we needed to know our own strengths and weaknesses. Her strengths complement my weaknesses and vice versa. In areas where we are equally strong, only one can drive the bus.

Before starting our Avon® business, we ran several other businesses together. One was another multi-level marketing company. While we did not exactly succeed, it prepared us for Avon.

"When life knocks you down, try to land on your back.
Because if you can look up, you can get up."
—Les Brown, American author and motivational speaker

Having the Wind Taken from Your Sail

I guess for the same reason our parents wanted to be the captain of their own ships, we too strived for that independence.

Three years prior to Avon, we started a wholesale business called KLM (Kendall Loves Maria). KLM was a wholesale tobacco business where we serviced accounts across about one third of Texas. We also opened and operated two retail locations. In our third year of business, KLM was doing a little more than $3,000,000 in sales.

You may wonder why we would stop doing that business to start a "little Avon thing." Imagine being in your office opening your mail and finding yourself holding a little more than $60,000 worth of useless checks that customers had written to us for product, that had bounced. In a traditional business, the risks of doing business can be enormous. Trust me when I say, waking up to that kind of loss will change your world!

Full Circle

It is strange how life can come full circle. It was a three-hour drive between our retail stores. I operated one and Maria ran the other along with the wholesale. We were working anywhere from 16 to 18 hours a day, 6 days a week. The only time we saw each other was on Sundays.

One day, a customer came through the drive-through and handed me an Avon brochure and asked me to give it to my wife. Wow, I could not recall the last time I had seen an Avon brochure.

When I came home, I gave Maria the brochure. Keep in mind, I have a wife, three daughters, two daughters-in-law and a mother-in-law. Imagine what kind of order they could put together (around $400). Maria said, "I can remember my mother selling Avon. No, wait—she signed up and I sold Avon." Her family had moved into a neighborhood where everyone only spoke English. Therefore, when they walked up to a door, Maria had to do the talking.

Never Let an Opportunity Pass You By

The next time the Avon representative who had given me the brochure came through the drive-through, I reluctantly handed her the order. I asked her if there was a fee to sign-up or if she would give us a discount because of the size of the order. How would you have answered that question? Just think; if one customer—like I— ordered that amount every campaign, you could make President's Recognition Program from just one customer!

Surprisingly, her reply was, "It looks like you are getting busy, so I'll get back with you later." When the next campaign came around, and because we loved Avon, we ordered about the same amount. I asked the same question and she avoided it again.

It seemed impossible, but a couple of days later, a customer went through Maria's drive-through and handed our son a brochure. Keep in mind that neither of us had seen an Avon brochure since we were young. Then, within a month's time, two people had given us books. God had a plan for us, we just did not know it yet.

Maria noticed a label on the back of the Avon brochure that said, "$10 to start." She picked up the phone and told the person who answered to come sign me up.

It was unfortunate for the first representative that she could only see how she would lose a great customer by signing us up. Had she taken the time to see the big picture, maybe we would do great things down the road. You have that same possibility with each and every person you sign up. If she had, then today she would be receiving a bonus check from our group, which did $1.5 million last year.

"Money is not everything but it ranks right up there with oxygen."
—Zig Ziglar, American author, salesman
and motivational speaker

Never, Never Prejudge

Maria's whole purpose of signing up with Avon was to buy at wholesale prices and save money on the orders family members placed for themselves. I can remember telling her I thought she was crazy for wanting to sign up. Our plate was full. We had no time to do something else.

Maria had just gotten started and had Avon materials sitting out at her store after her first appointment. A customer walked in and saw the materials. He picked up a brochure and asked, "Are you selling Avon?" When Maria asked him why, he went on to explain that his wife had told him to go ahead and order some Skin So Soft if he ever ran across an Avon representative, because they were almost out. Being the good businessperson she is, Maria responded, "Well, if you're buying, I'm selling!"

Conceive, Believe and Achieve

"What you can conceive and believe, you can achieve."
—Napoleon Hill, American author, journalist,
attorney and lecturer

I no longer thought Maria was crazy for signing up with Avon. We sold over $30,000 during the first year with the company. Plus, we never made a delivery. How is that possible? The customers we already had, who shopped our stores, placed and picked up their Avon orders when they came through the drive-throughs.

When Dana, our upline, was trying to make Senior Executive Unit Leader (SEUL), Maria decided to do Avon full time. This meant closing both her store and the wholesale. One thing tipped the scale for Maria's decision. The direct sales manager told Dana and Maria that they could not do it, that it had never been done before, and therefore it could not be done.

I will concede that helping Dana reach SEUL was a monster of a task. Dana needed to have six Unit Leaders (ULs), two of whom needed to be Executive Unit Leaders (EULs). To make matters worse, Dana only had five ULs at the time.

A little thing that all the naysayers did not know was that Dana had an ace in the hole. Someone telling Maria that she could *not* do something was like a red flag to a bull.

To pull it off, the team needed a lot of people to sign up. Therefore, they went out tailgating every day, *all* day. Some days were so long that it grew dark on them and they wrote up contracts by the light of a cell phone. On their best single day ever out tailgating, the team signed up 21 people.

By end of that campaign, they reached their goal. Dana became SEUL and Maria went from UL to EUL in one campaign—all within the first nine months as an Avon representative. If you want the impossible done, just tell Maria she cannot do it!

Just Luck?

It is always funny when I hear people say, "Oh, they are so lucky." Luck is when opportunity meets preparation. We had to go through certain life changing steps to be ready for when the opportunity showed up.

Sometimes you say to yourself, *Why am I going through the things I'm going through?* or *Why is this happening to me?* When you feel that way, just hold fast and keep your eye on the prize. If you do not waver, I promise you that somewhere down the road, when you look back at where you have been, you will see that it was not just a path you were going down. It was actually steps, one on top of another, each one preparing you for the next one.

The Secret

Ever since we made SEUL, people have asked us, "So, what is the secret to making Senior?" I truly do wish there were a secret to it. The truth is, there are no secrets to this business. No magic formula, no guarded handshake, no wonder pills. If there were a secret, I would share it with everyone! However, we have learned several success strategies we want to share with you.

Four Critical Strategies for Success

1. See and treat it as a business. It only cost $10 to start. How can that be a real business? Despite the low start-up cost, our business did $1.5 million in 2012. Hmmm—that kind of sounds like a real business to me! We work our business every day. It is not a hobby or "the make-up of the month club." See it as you want it to become, not where it is today.

2. Know your *why*. Understand why you are doing your business. It must be a big *why,* one that will keep you excited. It also must be selfish—not something for your kids. Sure, you will take care of them, with or without Avon, as you always have and I am sure you always will. If your reason for doing Avon is not big and exciting enough, then when you hit the first bump in the road, you will more than likely quit.

3. Let everyone know you sell Avon. That sounds simple, yet many representatives do not communicate it. Promote your business in every way, every day. When you do, people looking for a representative can find you. Do not hide behind just friends, family and coworkers. Look past your circle.

4. Never, never quit. The secret to success is that you never give up!

Now that you know our story, we hope you will use some of the tips we have learned for your own business. Remember that you can achieve what you imagine and believe you can. Discover and build on your strengths and take action as opportunities arise. Keep in mind the four strategies for success and there will be no stopping you. Our greatest wish is to see you at the top!

KENDALL CRONK &
MARIA DELGADO-CRONK

Avon® Senior Executive Unit Leaders
Avon Changing Lives Team
(817) 443-5332
avonyouandme@yahoo.com
www.facebook.com/
avonsignsanddecals

Maria has been self-employed, the pilot of her own destiny, since 2001. Prior to that, she worked in numerous jobs going back to her teenage years. She spent 15 years managing convenience stores.

With only an eighth grade education, and no general education, Maria managed to complete half of her teaching degree at a local college. Through Avon, Maria has the opportunity to teach, to train, and to show other women that no matter where they come from or what they have been through, they can achieve whatever they want in life.

Kendall has worked all his life, from hayfields to Corporate America, and many jobs in between. Growing up, he never saw himself having to work for someone else.

Dreams Do Come True!

BY PAM HELLER

We all have a window we look out each day. Our windows are all different due to life experiences and results from our past. Our past has great impact to what lies before us, decisions we make and believe in, and scope of what we are willing to dream for ourselves. We impact each other by our successes and failures. Often, this is evidence of what is and is not possible.

I am thankful for my past, the strength it has bestowed in me, and some of the hard decisions that were made by me or by others. These decisions have truly turned my life into something of a miracle, something beautiful. In contrast, life could have been dark, ugly and hopeless.

In this chapter I share with you five lessons I have learned in my journey to success in life and in business.

Lesson One: Don't Ever Give Up on Your Dream— Listen to Your Heart

I want to start with sharing a dream I have had since I was a very little girl. The dream was to meet, know, and have a relationship with my birth mother. You see, she was a victim of domestic violence and, despite attempts to leave with her two children, there came a survival moment when she just had to escape. I was about one year old at the time and grew up without ever knowing her. According to my father, "She was no good, just like all women are no good."

My childhood was turbulent and frightening. Jumping forth to the last straw, my father brought home his then live-in girlfriend from the hospital for a visitation with her children for a few hours. During this particular visit, there was a bad episode—she attempted suicide. Suddenly, he dragged her back to the hospital. Hours and hours passed. It appeared he was not coming home any time soon and I was left to my own devices. My brother and I ran amuck playing cowboys and Indians with my father's girlfriend's three children, raising all kinds of heck! The next thing we knew, there was a knock at the front door. Two police officers loaded us all into their car and took us to the police station.

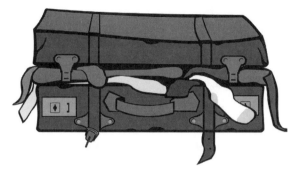

Authorities placed my brother and me in foster homes when I was 7 years old. I lived in foster care until age 17. I then attended business school for two years and married upon graduation at 19. My husband, John, was in the U.S. Army and we were stationed in Germany. At 21, I became pregnant with my daughter, Jessica.

I continued to dream of meeting my birth mother. Through encouragement from my foster mother, some researching and letter writing, my dream came true with a phone call one early morning. It was my mother on the other end of the line. Dreams do come true!

There will be many times in your business when you feel the goals and dreams you desire seem so far off in the distant future and almost impossible to achieve. I encourage you to expand your desire and focus on the end result. Break it down into smaller goals and milestones and work your plan in small segments. You have great potential—every one of us does. Find deep within you what you want. Do not give up and keep moving!

Lesson Two: Step Out of Your Comfort Zone and Execute

While overseas, I worked for the Army in a civilian capacity as a secretary. Working for generals, colonels and other staff officers, I gained great experience in many duties that are important for running a successful business. I am thankful for the skills this taught me:

- Organization
- Communication
- Follow-through
- Discipline
- Order
- Structure

As a military family, we moved often and I had to find new employment. It was exciting, yet frustrating, as any working military spouse or person who moves a lot will attest to. I have always loved working and getting things done. I have always been able to find joy in whatever type of work I have done, from cleaning horse stalls to working in clothing factories to greeting customers in a car dealership to supervising in a Sears® catalog department. My chosen profession was the secretarial field. I have always found work rewarding and satisfying, and even would say, I love to work!

A pivotal moment came when I worked in a position where my boss was mean and unpredictable. I became unhappy and a coworker suggested I start my own Avon® business. I revolted and disregarded her suggestion. In fact, I thought she was totally crazy—what was she thinking? She must have seen something in me that I did not. I was shy and I did not feel I had the confidence nor the competence to run my own business, much less to be a salesperson. There was just no way!

More time passed, and after many days driving home from work in tears, I decided I needed to break free of my situation—despite not wanting to leave my comfort zone. When you find yourself in a circumstance that makes you very unhappy and does not move you in the direction of your dreams, take a stand and draw that line in the sand. Vow to make a change for the better. Do it for your happiness and for your future. Allow yourself to be an example and inspire others. Exercise the free will God gave you.

I took a leap of faith, and with my husband's support and encouragement, I quit my job and went for it! I called Avon, paid my $20 for the start-up kit, signed on the dotted line and was on my way. I also gained a new, part-time secretarial position closer to my home. This assisted financially while building my business.

Although we had more bills than income, and the decision made no sense on paper, somehow I knew I had to do this. I would do whatever it took to make it work. After six months of working my business part-time, I was able to quit my other part-time job and convert my Avon business to full-time work.

My strategy was to sell Avon for "just a little while," until our bills were a little more manageable, and then quit Avon. I could potentially be a stay-at-home mom. We were living in Pennsylvania and my daughter was seven years old. I began dreaming about all the possibilities that working from home could bring. Never before had I even fathomed such a scenario.

Could this home-based business mean no more worrying about sick days for Jessica, school being cancelled due to snow, school vacation days, summers off, and having to beg for time off to match my husband's vacation days? I shudder just thinking about the twists and turns and the stress of making it all come together. Some amazing families can make this work, yet boy oh boy, it comes at a price.

Lesson Three: This Business Works if You Do

Could this also mean I might have the ability to volunteer at my daughter's school? How about the freedom to say, I won't ever miss my daughter's important life events. My husband had thirty vacation days a year in the military. I had one week and sometimes two, if I was lucky! Is it possible to have the best of both worlds—be there for your family when they need you and yet have a successful and thriving business? This started to feel like maybe it really could work. However, it was intimidating at the time and the income came slowly. I had a lot to learn.

Thankfully, I became fully engaged in the business and chose not to find excuses why I could not do it. Instead, I found reasons I could and ways to do it. I ran out the gate and got the business building.

I am thankful to have had many supportive and knowledgeable representatives and district and division sales managers. I made a point to immerse myself in every opportunity, incentive, and training meeting available. Sales meetings and conferences are especially important since surrounding yourself with like-minded individuals can transform processes and give you key ideas to impact your direction to build your business. Executing and working your ideas makes your business grow. Being consistent and moving your business, even a little at a time, makes a difference. Do not build haphazardly. Keep your momentum—it is everything!

When I tell you I had to make this work, I mean I had to! I was very diligent about paying our family bills. In no way would I allow my decision to impact our family finances in a negative way. I would do all in my power to make the correct decisions and use most of the time I had to create the profits necessary—no matter what. This was business!

The burning desire to succeed was breeding within me and the more I saw others succeed, the more I began to see the potential. I fell in love with Avon only a short time after discovering that I had the control to do or not do. The only one I had to answer to and lay claim to success or failure was me. Wow, what an opportunity! I was excited because I knew how much I enjoyed working and my willingness to give it all I had. I felt free—free to grow, to explore, to learn, to build and to earn in my business. My goal was to earn just $400 bi-weekly. If only I could achieve this income goal, I would be hugely satisfied.

This business works if you do. After all, Avon has been in business since 1886. It works. In fact, it works so well that today I earn over a six-figure income and still counting!

Lesson Four: This Business is Personal— Personal Development

It does not get more personal than relationships, does it? The single most important thing I have learned is the value of personal development. You must constantly be learning and exceeding your personal best. I have done this through attending seminars, reading books and listening to motivational speakers—both in and outside of Avon.

Learning about interpersonal skills and communication can make you a lot of money. The better you get at it, the more people you can impact and serve and the more potential business you can take on. Learn to get along with people and show interest in them to discover how you can best solve their problems and fill their needs. Most are quick to skim over this part and pounce. This is where you can shine and really excel! When you are interested in people, people will find you interesting!

Lesson Five: Plan, Schedule and Honor Yourself

It is exciting to create your business and go from nothing to a multi-million dollar business. Yes, it does take a bit more than "poof" and the business is built! Every day it takes small steps. It is the compounding of your efforts and the efforts of those you recruit that equals the growth you want.

Build your business on purpose and write it all down. Grab the calendar and decide when you are going to work and the hours you choose. It can be very flexible—the beauty of the business. Write out everything you must do to get your business humming, including:

- Find customers and new team members
- Submit orders
- Plan meetings
- Make follow-up phone calls
- Locate events to promote your business
- Deliver orders
- Send emails
- Connect on social media

Keep one project or To Do list. Select six to ten items and determine how much time each task takes and ink it in on your calendar. Plan one night a week with this process and watch your list whittle down and your self-esteem go up!

The tricky part is executing what you say you will do. This sounds easy, however I have noticed this can be the biggest trip-up. It is too easy, when you are your own boss, to say, *Oh, I'll do that tomorrow or I'll get to it eventually.* Do not fall for it! Get it on your calendar and keep appointments to do your tasks just as if you were going to meet with someone. Life happens and things come up. When they do, simply reschedule. It takes time to get in the habit, however gaining this discipline is worth it. You will thank yourself for being the best boss you ever had.

Time to Act Now!

Do you have a dream within you that you are not acting upon? Do not ever give up—focus to make your dream come to fruition! Life is not always easy and no one gets a hall pass. You will be uncomfortable at times, therefore get ready to move out of your comfort zone so you can move into a more satisfying future.

No matter who you are, where you come from, or how much money or education you have, this business can work for you! It is a matter of getting your mindset solid and becoming fully committed to your intention. Do not allow the distractions to get the best of you. When they do, recommit yourself.

You only have yourself, for the most part. No matter what, make yourself a priority and invest in yourself. Attend seminars, read books and listen to motivational speakers. These resources have shortcuts and ideas you can take advantage of to lessen frustrations and speed up your journey to your goals. They also help build your belief and confidence during your journey.

My business brings me great gratification—the ability to empower others to enhance their quality of life, whether it is financial, personal or relationship related. I enjoy bringing families together, helping moms be able to stay home with their babies, and helping others raise their level of self-confidence.

Thousands upon thousands of Avon representatives and employees have come before us, building the business to what it is today. We are all part of the legacy of those coming after us. It is a remarkable feeling being part of an organization that does so much for so many, from an income opportunity to supporting breast cancer and domestic violence foundations.

I am fortunate to have learned from many others. I am grateful to have great customers and a fantastic team of representatives with whom I have the privilege of partnering.

Begin and act on your plan and you will succeed. Step by step and day by day, your business will continue to grow at the speed you do. If you have a down day, reflect on the beginning when you started and had no customers, team members, or knowledge of where you were taking the business when you started. This reflection gives you a point of reference for what you have accomplished so you do not feel defeated on those days of blunder. Always remember to honor yourself and follow through and do what you say you are going to do.

Success is yours!

PAM HELLER

Avon® Senior Executive Unit Leader
Rose Circle Member
DSWA Certified Elite Leader
Avon Products
www.pamheller.com
(800) 774-3730
avonbysell@aol.com

Pam was born in Allentown, Pennsylvania, and grew up in the foster care system. She attended Churchman Business School and graduated with a degree in specialized business. Pam and her husband, John, have been married since 1984 and work their Avon business together in South Carolina.

Pam began her Avon journey in 1993 and today runs a multi-million dollar business out of her living room with more than 1,000 team members. She is a compassionate leader and mentor with a goal of having ten of her leaders reach the Senior level and have personal earnings of one million.

Pam has been featured in Avon's *Women in the Spotlight* and *Success Without Limits* DVDs and in *Empowering Women Magazine*. Pam is a member of the Direct Selling Women's Alliance and a featured author in the organization's *Build It Big II* book. She has received many awards and achieved numerous incentive trips.

Pam and John's daughter, Jessica, graduated with honors from the University of South Carolina and pursues her own Avon business full-time. Pam prides herself in being able to work closely with her daughter in both business and life.

Make Success Attainable: Working Strategically to Grow Quickly

BY ROSEMARIE OSOLINSKY

When you are just starting out in multi-level marketing, the highest levels of success can seem far out of reach. However, achieving your dreams is possible and the pace is something you can control. Plan your success one step at a time by setting small, reachable, targeted goals. Do not let the fear of failure limit your dreams. Embrace setbacks as part of the process.

The first time I signed up to sell Avon®, I was 19 and did not sell much more than the demos I bought for myself. At 38, I decided to give my Avon business another try. My husband and I were struggling to raise our two young children, Lydia and Will, on a tight budget and Avon gave me play money to go on vacation or take my kids to the movies. It was not until I was 48 years old that I decided to make Avon and leadership my career.

Although I was working a full-time job and our family was making enough money to get by, I was seeing signs all around that I needed to make some changes. My husband's job gave us a steady income, however it was so stressful that his coworker had a heart attack on the job and died at his desk. At the same time, my children—then ages 12 and 16—were at a point in their lives when they needed more hands-on guidance. I needed to do something drastic. I had to take a risk that could lift my family up, give us the security of financial stability and the freedom of financial independence.

I decided to quit my job. I talked it over with my husband, Bill, who agreed it was a good move for our family. It was a calculated risk in that I had met people who were successful with Avon, making over $100,000 in the leadership program. Therefore, I knew that it was indeed possible to make Avon a lucrative career. I also knew I could count on the company to be a reliable business partner because it had been in business for over 100 years.

Nevertheless, deciding and doing are two different things. When the day came to quit my regular job and sign up to sell Avon, Bill had second thoughts. After all, we were doing okay. We had saved a little money and had some put away for our daughter to start college the following year. However, I knew I could do better; that I could teach and mentor a team of representatives and that together we would all have a better life. My frustration became unbearable and I took the stack of books from our kitchen table and threw them on the floor. *It's too late!* I yelled. *You will not deny me this opportunity!* This anger, this intensity, this passion, was so undeniably profound that my husband decided to support my decision and has supported it ever since.

We risked everything. We cashed out both of our retirement accounts to live on until my Avon earnings kicked in. We also purchased a car for me to run the business. This left us vulnerable, which only added to my devotion to my Avon business. I needed to make this work—and fast.

It was not always easy, and the beginning years were lean. After working day and night for months with my team, I received a leadership check for just $175. I was devastated. All of my work and effort for $175, for two full weeks of work! It was hard to take. I vented to Bill that, despite my hard work, I just was not seeing cash results and I wanted to give up. This time I saw the passion in *his* eyes. He looked at me and said, "Don't you ever say that. You *have* to make it!" That was a turning point for me. Failure was not an option. I had more than time and effort invested in this. My family was counting on me.

Here are my earnings from my first years in Avon Leadership:

YEAR	EARNINGS
1	$4,700
2	$43,000
3	$74,000
4	$89,000
5	$129,000
6	$166,000
7	$200,000

This is my 13th year as a leadership representative and I have earned almost $2,000,000 total. Each year, my earnings have climbed significantly, and I am proud to say that I have made over $200,000 a year with my Avon business for the past seven years. As you can see, I did make it.

Avon has changed our lives. Within three years of starting my business, Bill's company closed and we had sufficient income from Avon to move to where we wanted—not where his job dictated. We chose Phoenix, Arizona, where my mother and brothers lived.

We have remodeled our home, both inside and out, and we even installed a putting green in our back yard. I enjoy having my coffee each morning while watching Bill chip golf balls over the swimming pool onto the green and looking at my Avon trophies, which I display in our cactus garden. I know it may seem odd to keep them there, but it is the best showcase I can imagine. This is truly the house that Avon built. Or, I should say, that we built together.

In addition, we put our children through college without student loans, both of whom went on to get master's degrees. We have also been able to be much more charitable and give to our church and to people in need.

Avon has also given us the freedom to travel, which meant a lot to me when my son was in school. He was on the football team at the University of Texas at El Paso and we were able to go to every game—more than fifty of them—all across the country. In addition, because I am a top achiever, Avon has sent me to many spectacular destinations all around the world. Through the company, I have traveled to Australia, Spain, France, Monaco, Italy, Mexico, Canada, the Bahamas, Alaska, Hawaii, San Francisco, San Diego, Miami, Key West and Las Vegas.

How I Got to Where I Am

Everything begins with a goal. Because I quit my job to pursue a career with Avon, and we depleted our savings in order for me to do so, I needed to make up my income quickly. To do this, I needed a massive push to jump-start my team. I set a two-part goal:

1. To recruit 100 new representatives to my team, any generation, in three months

2. To be a Senior Executive Unit Leader (SEUL) making $100,000 a year within five years

I started by making a warm list of possible business contacts, just like we do with new representatives during their initial appointment. I listed everyone I could think of—professional women, stay-at-home mothers, old, young, with a job, without a job—everyone. This gave me a starting point. From there, I made contact with them and set appointments to share my earning opportunity. If they were not interested in selling, they would be my customers.

I started a log and numbered it from 1 to 100. Each day, as new representatives were appointed, I wrote their names into the next numbered slots, along with their account numbers, phone numbers, campaign of appointments, and upline representatives. I also kept track of order sizes for their first four campaigns and a record of my communication attempts.

Because my group was small, I was able to follow up with all representatives for their first four campaigns, no matter what generation. By creating relationships with these representatives, I increased the chances that they would succeed with Avon. At the same time, it helped me to identify the achievers who could be my future leaders.

Duplication

One of my first leaders was a disabled nurse who babysat my kids and was looking for financial independence. We began her team just as I did mine, with the warm list. I took her by the hand and together we went prospecting, appointing and recruiting. She soon became a Unit Leader. Because she was new and still learning, I mentored her and her new representatives at the same time. I went with her on every call, to initial appointments as well as follow-up. Even though today she is an SEUL, I am still there to support both her and her team. I am available to coach and guide people in my downline, regardless of their titles. All I ask is that each individual wants to grow and is willing to do the work to get there.

When we lead by example, we duplicate ourselves. Today I have over 2,300 representatives, many of whom are supporting their families and fulfilling their dreams through their Avon businesses. Six of those are SEULs and nine are Executive Unit Leaders (EULs), which shows that they are not only great representatives, but also great leaders who are continually growing.

Communication

As my team grew, I worked to create spaces for training and support. I found regular, targeted meetings to be highly effective. Keep in mind that meetings can be any size, from one-on-one conversations to large group classes. I recommend that each meeting always include three components: recognition, training, and a call to action. Each of these work together to help the representative leave with a renewed sense of excitement and clarity on how to achieve her goals.

1. Recognition: Acknowledge what the representative has done well. Along with applauding the obvious, recognize her specifically for the behavior you emphasize in that particular meeting. For example, recognize for title advancement, for new candidates under a representative, for a number of appointments, for first orders with new downline, for an increase in personal sales, or even for the behaviors necessary for the new candidate or appointment. This could be the number of times a representative went out recruiting or that they took Beauty of Knowledge training courses on youravon.com.

2. Training: Every contact with your downline representatives is a teaching opportunity. Materials, like a handout, can be very helpful and increase the likelihood that the representative will retain the new information and be able to share what she learned with her downline representatives and/or customers. Always tailor materials to the representative's present sales or leadership position.

3. A Call to Action: Leave your representative with a clear idea of what immediate steps to take toward meeting goals.

Keep in mind that communication is not one-sided, therefore it is important to listen. When you hear the representative's goals, your coaching will be relevant to her. If you are not speaking about what matters to her, chances are she is not hearing you, either.

At its root, communication with your team is best done with the goal of building relationships. You are asking people to believe and trust you when you say this business can change their lives; therefore it is important for them to know you and your values. I see my downline as family and feel a responsibility to help them as much as I possibly can. This means pushing myself to learn new ways to teach, different ways to motivate, and better ways to lead.

My Current Goals

My personal goals today are to be more active in my church, buy a second home in California to be closer to my daughter and her family, and eventually to have us all together in the same area.

My long-term business goal is to double my income within the next ten years. The easiest way to do this is through duplication. I will need six new SEULs. I must continue to build my first generation and look within my present group for high potential representatives to work with while still encouraging my present leaders. I am always looking for someone I can support on her journey—someone who has a dream, a strong work ethic, a caring personality, and who is coachable and ethical. Just as I have done with my current leaders, I will guide them through and be at their side as they come into their own. I will be a hands-on participant in their success.

My goals are steep, as they always have been. Looking back at everything I did to make my team grow and prosper helps me remember the unlimited potential of Avon leadership, as well as my own potential. I am ready to do it all over again.

> *"The greater danger for most of us lies not in setting our aim*
> *too high and falling short; but in setting our aim too low,*
> *and achieving our mark."*
> **—Michelangelo, Italian sculptor, painter, architect and poet**

Goals Determine the Pace of Success

Set short-term targets that are both challenging and achievable, as well as long-term dreams to keep you going. How hard you push yourself and how quickly are within your control.

Goals are only effective if coupled with the right motivation. If you have a clear sense of your *why*—the reason you do what you do— you can build your goals around this and be as effective as possible. It is the catalyst that makes you stretch beyond your comfort zone, work harder, and try something new. By defining your *why* you can establish the steps you need to get there and you can help others define theirs.

ROSEMARIE OSOLINSKY

Avon® Senior Executive Unit Leader
Avon Products

(602) 573-9153
rosolinsky@yahoo.com
www.youravon.com/rosolinsky

Rosemarie sold Avon at ages 19 and 36, then returned to the company at 48 with renewed passion and a goal. She quickly set the record for growth by achieving Senior Executive Unit Leader in only ten months. Rosemarie leads a team of over 2,300 representatives. In 2013, she received the Woman of Enterprise award.

With over $8,000,000 in unit sales, Rosemarie ranks fourth in the Nation and first in the Western Region. She has sold at every level of achievement from President's Club to Inner Circle and was the first representative recognized at a national event for achieving both SEUL and Inner Circle. Rosemarie specializes in working with representatives to help them achieve their goal and, in 2012, was the only representative chosen by Avon to go to Australia to share her insight on growing a leadership business. She was also chosen to speak at the Avon 2010 Worldwide Finance Conference in San Francisco.

Rosemarie has been featured in *Beauty Fashion Magazine, Empowering Women Magazine, Avon Dreams,* and the book *What It Takes...To Earn $1,000,000 In Direct Sales* by Kristen McCay-Smith, published by 50 Interviews Inc., 2009. To join Rosemarie's team go to www.startavon.com, reference code: rosolinsky.

Dream, Believe, Achieve

BY CHRIS AND GINGERMICHELE KAPP

*"Every one of us is born with unlimited potential, we have
the ability and intelligence to make the impossible possible.
Remember, the only person that can hold you back in life is yourself,
you just can't dream it, you must believe that you have
the power to achieve it."*
—Author Unknown

I have been called many names, but I never thought "Avon® Lady"
would have been one of them.

I often feel that I have lived life with my back against the wall—from
facing constant challenges with family to health issues to frequent
moving—and you may relate. Yet it was the bullying that really
drove me.

From an early age, I am sad to say, that I experienced the hate that
children, young adults and even family can inflict upon each other.

As much as it hurt, I tried not to let it get to me. In fact, it was the very thing that guided me. Without knowing specifically what I wanted to do in life, I knew from a young age that I wanted to help others. I wanted to turn my hurt into a positive and make other people feel good about themselves—and I wanted to prove the naysayers wrong!

"Go ahead, tell me that I'm not good enough. Tell me I can't do it, because I will show you over and over again that I can!"
—Author Unknown

Early Family Life

I met my husband and now Avon business partner, Chris, in tenth grade. Through my tumultuous high school years, he was my rock—and still is! At age 17, I graduated from high school. Shortly after I turned 18, we became proud parents of a beautiful little girl, September Sapphire, in 1998. Soon thereafter, Chris joined the Navy in 1999. While he was in A-school, we got married. His military adventure is what would lead me to my life's calling.

While stationed at our first duty station, I worked a couple of different J.O.B.s and even tried out a home-based business opportunity, Mary Kay®. In 2001, just two days after 9/11, we had our second child, Gabriele Celebrity Athena, another beautiful little girl.

It goes without saying that life is full of ups and downs. Military life—living in an unfamiliar city with two young children, a husband who often deploys, and living paycheck-to-paycheck is a rollercoaster. I also found myself in a disagreement with my parents, who felt like we could not handle these circumstances. I needed to show them otherwise—quickly!

"Don't let the things that matter most be at the mercy of those that matter least."
—Johann Wolfgang von Goethe, German writer and politician

Shortly after moving to our second duty station, my husband came home one day and handed me an Avon® book that he found hanging on our door. I was thrilled to see it, as I had not seen one in years! My mother and grandma used to buy Avon and I remember them letting my cousin and me play with the makeup, fragrances and jewelry. I immediately sat down and started making an order. When I called the number on the back, I found out that the representative was my neighbor who just moved in.

A few months later, my representative called me to ask if I could help her out at the local county fair. She explained that her team member had canceled. Of course I said yes—I love going to the fair. While I was assisting her at the fair, I met three people who expressed interest in joining Avon.

I saw just how simple it was to work an Avon business, as opposed to the other home-based business I was with. On the way home, I asked her questions about the business. When she told me it was just $10 to get started, I thought two things; *Sign me up* and *My Husband is going to kill me!* When we arrived home, I ran inside my house to get the $10 and quickly went next door to sign up. I was excited—enough to appoint three new representatives the very same day I joined!

I became Unit Leader in my first campaign and earned the $300 Fast Start Bonus. I thought, *Finally, I may have a platform for a proper future for myself and my family, and the resolve that I feel to help others.*

A Big Picture Person

Although the fast start in Avon was exciting to me, it was what I learned later that kept me engaged. Naturally, I was happy to earn a leadership check. My first was a whopping $11! It was a start and I felt valued. Moreover, I felt a sense of community. Women—and a few good men— partnering together to help each other. Couple that with thorough training and incredible recognition and I was hooked.

Moving on Up

Chris and I earned our first Avon trip in 2005, a Bahamas cruise. When we returned home, he was completely on board to help and support me with my business. I decided it was time to take our business to the next level. The following year, we earned another Bahamas cruise. I partnered with my team to help them achieve their goals and I advanced to Advanced Unit Leader (AUL). With so much momentum, I again advanced—only two campaigns later—to Executive Unit Leader (EUL).

"If you want happiness for a lifetime—help someone else."
—Chinese proverb

Fight for What You Believe In!

Once again, we found ourselves moving to our third duty station in 2006. We never could have imagined what 2007 had in store for us. Chris's military career came to an end and we found ourselves trying to re-learn how to live in the civilian world again. We also were dealing with my parents wanting to invoke their grandparent's rights to have custody of our children. Despite wanting to run away from it all, I knew that Avon was now our only income and we needed to give ourselves a raise.

We sprang into action despite the circumstances we faced. During the last campaign before Christmas, we were close to our goal and our hard work was paying off. We met my parents to drop off our girls before Christmas, as agreed upon, whether we liked it or not, and headed home to complete our last minute customer holiday deliveries. When we finished them all, we could not help thinking that it was not right not being able to have Christmas with our kids, grandparent's rights or not. We had never before missed a Christmas together and at that moment, I made up my mind that we never would.

Instantly, we packed and jumped into our car to head north, not letting anyone know. Arriving Christmas morning, we called our girls to say "Merry Christmas" and to ask when they would be going to my grandparents' house to open their presents. Once they were there, we opened the door and surprised everyone. At last we were together for Christmas! The next day, we found out that we had achieved Senior Executive Unit Leader (SEUL). What an amazingly overwhelming great feeling!

> *"Some people succeed because they are destined to, but most people succeed because they are determined to."*
> **—Henry Ford, American founder of Ford Motor Company, father of modern assembly lines**

In 2008, we celebrated our success in Las Vegas for a week at the Bellagio and even got to meet Sarah Ferguson and Suze Orman.

In May 2011, I participated in the Walk the Course Against Domestic Violence Event in Charlotte, North Carolina. Our Avon team was made up of representatives and district managers from the Cherokee Division. We were the top fundraising team. For five miles, I was not only improving my health by walking, I was also reflecting on the lives I was helping. I was so proud to be a part of this. The next year, our team photo was featured in an Avon brochure. What an honor!

Sometimes Even the Best Fall Down

We experienced setbacks and distractions along the way. We became complacent and even fell back to EUL. Again, we partnered with our team and worked hard to regain SEUL status.

> *"It's not how many times you get knocked down that counts,*
> *it's how many times you get back up."*
> —**Vince Lombardi, American football player, coach**
> **and executive**

The year 2013 has been incredible for us. We took our kids to Disney World® and Universal® Studios. We took a weekend getaway to Chicago for our anniversary and a week in Hawaii. We never thought we would have been able to do any of this. We achieved President's Council and are thankful every day for our wonderful customers and incredible team that continues to amaze me and keep me motivated!

Dream Big

Our business has been amazing to us! We have no debt and are no longer living paycheck to paycheck. We are now saving to buy our dream home with a horse farm and for a trip to Paris! One day, we even plan to buy our dream cars, a blue Ferrari® for me and a 1970 Cuda® for Chris. We have since resolved our differences with my parents. I truly believe our Avon business has changed our lives and the lives of the people with whom we have come in contact. I have completely come out of my shell and am even learning to speak in front of an audience.

"Do one thing every day that scares you."
**—Eleanor Roosevelt, American former First Lady
of the United States**

Tips for Success

*"People don't care how much you know until they know
how much you care."*
**—John C. Maxwell, American evangelical Christian author,
speaker and pastor**

Throughout my journey with Avon, I have learned strategies that have helped in my success. I believe these can work for you, too.

- **Do not just be an order taker.** Listen to people's needs and personalize your service. One of the most important things I have learned is that this is a relationship business.
- **Learn your team members' emotional *why*.** Remind them of it often.
- **Assume the sale.** You have just what they need, be it products or opportunity.
- **Always be honest.** Honesty is the best policy. If you are unsure of an answer, do not be afraid to say, *That's a great question, I'm going to find out and get back to you.*
- **Offer sincere compliments.** A sincere compliment or gesture can change a person's entire day, put a smile on her face, and make you both feel good. This is also a great way to talk to her about Avon.
- **Do not worry about what other people think of you.** Keep on shining, because you are doing something right!
- **Do not give up** just because of what someone said or did to you. Use that as motivation to push harder and prove him or her wrong!

"Energy and persistence conquer all things."
**—Benjamin Franklin, American founding father of the
United States, leading author, politician, scientist and inventor**

- **Reinvest back into your business.** I try to do one or more events every month, and even more as it gets closer to the holidays. Fairs are my favorite way to get in front of a lot of people, especially since that is how I got my start.
- **Lead by example.** Take a team member with you for "hip time." Attach her to your hip and let her hear the words you use when talking to potential customers and recruits. Duplication is key.
- **Utilize all of the tools Avon offers.**
- **Start each day with an inspirational quote.**
- **Become a master prospector.** This is the lifeline of our business. Find out what works best and run with it. Anytime, anywhere, always ask! If you do not ask, the answer is always no.
- **Follow up.** Be consistent and never give up!
- **Know your goal.** Keep it in front of you at all times. A constant reminder is to create a dream board that is regularly viewable.
- **Plan for success.** Then put your plan into action.

Did You Know:
- 48 percent of sales people never follow up with a prospect
- 25 percent of sales people make a second contact and stop
- 12 percent of sales people make more than three contacts
- 2 percent of sales are made on the first contact
- 3 percent of sales are made on the second contact
- 5 percent of sales are made on the third contact
- 10 percent of sales are made on the fourth contact
- 80 percent of sales are made on the fifth to twelfth contact

Social Media

Stay in front of your prospects at all times. I utilize Facebook® a lot. I ask everyone I meet if they have Facebook. If I can get people to like my page or add me as a friend, they can see everything I post. I make sure to share consistently about my success. Eventually, if it was not the right time in their lives when I first met them, something might have changed and they later become interested in finding out more. If you do not have a Facebook or another type of social media, set up an account today and connect with me at www.facebook.com/gingermichele.kapp.

"Our goals can only be reached through a vehicle of a plan, in which we must fervently believe, and upon which we must vigorously act. There is no other route to success."
—Pablo Picasso

If you have a dream, protect it at all costs. Always fight for what you believe in and in no time you will achieve success. I'll see you soon, at the top!

CHRIS AND GINGERMICHELE KAPP

Avon® Senior Executive Unit Leaders
President's Council
Team Dream, Believe, Achieve
1-800-789-0098
gkapp.avon@gmail.com
www.youravon.com/gkapp
www.startavon.com, code: gkapp

Chris and Gingermichele Kapp are high school sweethearts from York, Pennsylvania. They both graduated in 1998 from York County School of Technology. Gingermichele studied graphic arts & printing and Chris studied auto body repair. Chris joined the Navy in 1999 and they married later that year. They have two daughters. They have lived in Beaufort, South Carolina, since 2006.

Since getting their start with Avon in 2003, Chris and Gingermichele have been featured in the *Representative Times,* in the PRP booklet, on youravon.com and in the Avon brochure. They have achieved President's Club or above every year since 2004. Chris and Gingermichele are at the top in recruiting and sales in their district. They received the Spirit of Avon Award in 2008. Together, Chris and Gingermichele run an over one million dollar business.

Gingermichele is one of the youngest Senior Executive Unit Leaders in the company and also sells at the President's Council level. She is also a Certified Beauty Advisor. Gingermichele enjoys helping others, spending time with family, horseback riding, dancing, listening to music, watching movies, traveling and trying out new restaurants.

Photo by: Kristi James

Reach Your Potential to Make Your Dreams Come True

BY ROSA DE LA O GOMEZ

When I was 12 years old growing up in Mexico, I started using my aunt's Odyssey cologne spray, powder, skin softener and my favorite—the Rollette. I had no idea that one day I would answer a local ad and eventually sustain my family with an Avon® business.

As a child, I started dreaming from the moment I noticed other children in my neighborhood receiving toys for Christmas, while my siblings and I were not. When April 30th rolled around and Mexico celebrated Día del Niño, or Day of the Child, we watched empty-handed as other children received gifts.

At age 13, my parents divorced. I promised myself that when I grew up, my children would have the things I did not have as a child, even if that meant holding two full-time jobs. A stable family was also part of my plan for adulthood. Some of the many thoughts that went through my head at such a young age were, *Why was I born to a poor family? Why did the other children have things we did not?* and *Why are they happy and we are not?*

Today, I understand that we all have a choice to determine how we spend our days and that each day is full of opportunities. I have overcome many obstacles on the road to success.

My husband, David, grew up in the United States. He was on an extended visit to his family in Mexico while I was studying hospitality management in college. When I began working at a hotel, I met David, who was also working there. We became good friends and fell in love. However, David missed the United States. He reluctantly said good-bye and traveled back. Once home, David asked me to join him in the United States. I agreed and left my home in Mexico. Soon afterward, we got married. Our first child, Margarita, was born and I became a stay-at-home mom.

An Unexpected New Journey

In August 1990, when Margarita was one year old, my mother-in-law asked me to make a call for her about how to become an Avon representative. However, I did not speak English and the person who answered the phone did not speak Spanish. The woman told me that someone would contact me in a few hours. She had a Spanish-speaking person call me back. I provided my address and we set up an appointment for her to come by and explain the details. My first impression was that the company provides good service!

My mother-in-law said that she would sign up and I would be her helper. The Avon representative arrived, however my mother-in-law did not. When I called her to let her know the representative was there to sign her up, she told me my father-in-law was not able to bring her. She said that I should sign up and she would be my helper. My answer was, "Absolutely not!"

I apologized to the representative and explained that the person interested in Avon could not be there. That is when she suggested I try it myself and give Avon a chance. "Don't you need money?" she asked. I came up with plenty of excuses. I did not know anyone and had no friends or family. I did not speak English or drive a car. I did not have $8.50 to pay for the contract. The representative suggested that I charge the fee to the account on my first order.

My husband was not going to like the idea of me selling Avon. He worked in construction and would come home tired from work. The representative was anxious for me to sign the contract by the time she left. She encouraged me and told me it would be easy. She explained that I would be able to continue taking care of my baby and remain a homemaker. I started to like the idea of making money again. In Mexico, I had worked full-time. However, I had never sold anything before. I was terrified of talking to strangers. Despite my concerns, I signed the contract to become an Avon representative.

Overcoming My Fears

I went to the laundry room near my apartment and gave a brochure to a woman there. I was scared and walked away, but she stopped me and said she wanted to buy Avon products! My first order was $94 with three customers—including my "helper," my mother-in-law.

Now I was worried about how I would find customers for the next order. I was determined to be successful and spent hours studying the brochure. It occurred to me to start calling people from the phonebook. It was difficult to make thirty to fifty calls a day and only acquire three to five appointments for the weekend. I remember pausing in between calls, crying because some people were nastily asking why I was bothering them while they were sleeping.

Eventually, I learned that the best time to make cold calls was between 3:00 and 6:00 p.m. Because I could not speak English, I chose Spanish last names in the phone book. I looked for people located within a ten-mile radius, as I depended on my husband to take me to my appointments. I brought brochures and samples and began to gain more customers.

The language barrier proved to be a challenge in other ways too. David had to read me the invoices because they were in English, as were the brochures. My district sales manager did not speak Spanish. I went to sales meetings and sat with the bilingual representatives, interrupting them to find out what people were discussing in the meeting.

I took inspiration from Avon publications featuring top sellers with sales surpassing $550,000. I told David we could make my dreams come true with Avon.

Every day, I fell more in love with Avon. I saw how much I could earn, however David did not agree and told me it would be impossible. In fact, he decided to try another business and I found myself putting my dream on standby. I left Avon for awhile to give David and his business endeavor my full support. I told him if we wanted to be successful, we would have to dedicate to just one business.

The other company required a $3,000-a-month investment. This was money we did not have so David took out loans. In just three months, we lost our home. We were stuck with a huge debt and many boxes of products. For the next six months, we found ourselves renting rooms here and there. David lost his job and we barely had enough money to put food on the table.

Believing in Avon

My district sales manager convinced me to return to Avon. She was the only one who believed in my potential. I persuaded David by expressing how I had supported him in trying make a success of his business and now I was asking him to give me a chance at mine. I still believed in Avon.

David gave me two months to prove that we could earn enough money through Avon to pay for our basic needs. He agreed—with many stipulations like, "My sleep is sacred," "I won't burn my brain thinking how this will work," and "It's your responsibility to figure out how to plan, just tell me what to do." He reminded me that he was not a sales person and would not knock on doors. If my Avon business did not work, David would go back to construction.

That night, I did not sleep and saw the sun rise. I was tired, yet eager to start working my plan. It was all written down, my dreams and goals, including David's role which included distributing brochures and helping me with deliveries.

Growing Sales

The first step was to invest in 500 brochures. My plan began to work. People started calling and saying, "I haven't seen an Avon Brochure in so long. Thank you!" It was as if they were cheering me on. We reinvested our earnings by purchasing 1,000 brochures. In just a few campaigns, we were buying up to 5,000 brochures. The mass distribution brought us sales averaging $7,000 per campaign. Our biggest sale in one campaign was $11,000.

The response was incredible. My business education allowed me to become a good administrator. First we paid off our debt. We also participated in an incentive and earned enough points to furnish our entire apartment!

David became a true believer when we bought our first new car. He admits that his biggest fear was that people would call him an Avon Lady! Now he displays those words on his license plate. It no longer bothers him because, as he says of himself, "I became a somebody and my friends respect that. I am the father my daughter wants me to be, participating at school and making her proud."

In 1995, we moved into our first home, a two-bedroom condominium. One room was for our daughter and the other was for our Avon business. David and I slept in the living room. However, we were happy knowing that every check was bringing us closer to my dream house.

In 2000, our sales volume was $163,415. In 2002, we were able to move to a second house and three years later, my dream house became a reality.

I had it custom built with a floor plan that had to fulfill my expectations. I chose it to have a lot of space, two-car garage, fireplace, enough bedrooms to receive visitors, walk-in closets, a dining room, two-story family room and foyer, master bath with a Jacuzzi®, studio/office space, large kitchen, panoramic windows, and walk-out basement.

From Sales to Leadership

When Avon began its leadership program in the 1990's, our main focus was sales. We were eager to become Private Circle honorees. That all changed when we attended the first Avon convention in 1999 and met Lisa Wilber, who opened our eyes. Lisa showed us her leadership earnings and told us that support was the most important ingredient for growing our downline. At that point, we had about 115 representatives in our first generation.

We knew we had to restructure our business approach. One of our strategies was to convert many of our 84 helpers and 800 customers into independent Avon representatives. We began teaching them to sell and recruit. We coached them to reinvest their earnings in their business and to buy brochures in bulk. We explained how they can open an exclusive Avon bank account and put money aside to pay Avon. For sales, we encouraged our representatives to take advantage of the Beauty of Knowledge online training, assist at the district beauty seminars, and attend sales meetings.

Searching for potential leaders in our team requires patience and vision. We use the eighty/twenty rule. Identify that twenty percent committed to working as a team and give them the tools and support needed for them to develop their skills.

I consider myself a disciple of *John Maxwell,* an internationally respected leadership expert, speaker and author. I read books about leadership to David on the way to our Avon training center. We created "Training for Trainers" for Executive Unit Leaders (EULs) and Senior Executive Unit Leaders (SEULs). We motivate them to achieve higher titles by showing them how to plan. We mutually commit to achieving their goals and give ourselves time to nurture our relationship, to train, to guide and help them plan short-, mid- and long-term goals, and to celebrate each achievement.

It is about trust and teamwork. David and I are passionate about helping everyone achieve the American Dream. We are both grateful to Avon for providing us with this tremendous opportunity and the tools that help us achieve our dreams and goals. We are continuously working closely with our Avon family—our team—to help them achieve all the incentives.

I have found my talents and David has also found his. We have discovered that we can positively influence people by sharing our expertise and knowledge acquired from many years in business. It goes much deeper than the financial outcome. We want to help others discover what they can achieve.

In the last five years, a bad time in the United States economy, we have been able to give ourselves a raise every year.

In all our years with Avon, we have 1,200 representatives in our downline, from which 4 of our leaders have become SEULs. Our plan is to develop at least 18 SEULs in the next 8 years. We have earned national trips 20 years in a row.

The Desire to Serve Others

Ever since I was 12, I have been losing important people in my life— my father, because I do not know if he is still alive, my mother's parents, who gave me my education, and the most painful one, my mother passing and not being able to be at her funeral. For two years after my mother's passing, a question tortured my being—why did I lose my loved ones without the chance to see them again?

I came to the United States to form a beautiful family. I achieved many materialistic goals I had set my mind to. I have nurtured friends, whom I call my second family, through my Avon business. Yet I knew there must be a stronger reason to be here. I prayed to God for the answer.

One day, while having breakfast with my husband at McDonald's®, I witnessed a wonderful act of kindness. I could not resist shedding a tear. There, in front of me, sat a male vagabond and beside him, a female vagabond. When she got up to get something, I saw him take out a $10 bill and place it on her table. At that moment, I realized that if a beggar can share the very little he has, why is it that we, who have been blessed with more, are not doing acts of kindness?

I discovered the reason why I am here. I want to dedicate every day of my life to every human being I come across. I am thankful to God because my life is full of blessings, even if I have lost many people in my life. Every time I find someone who decides to challenge themselves with the Avon opportunity, I find myself part of their life and their success. I share the passion we have for our business so they may apply it to theirs. We share the methods that have worked for us in the past so they do not have to reinvent the wheel. Our commitment is for everyone who wants to succeed in life.

It is a privilege to be able to influence people you have only just met. We have progressed from dreamers to drivers of dreams. The great thing is that people will always dream, and we want to be there to help their dreams come true.

It is time for you to take action. If I can achieve this kind of success, so can you. Commit to your goals, take control of your finances, and be determined. With focus and perseverance, you can make it to the top!

ROSA DE LA O GOMEZ
Avon® Senior Executive Unit Leader

(703) 379-1717
rdavon2005@msn.com
www.youravon.com/rdelao

Rosa and her husband, David, live in Woodbridge, Virginia. They have been married since 1997 and have three children, Margarita, Devean Jelani, and Joseph David.

Rosa was born in Mexico, where she studied hospitality management and worked in a hotel. She began her Avon business in 1990. Rosa has been featured in several publications, including *Broadband House Magazine, Representative Times* and *What's New*. Her lifetime achievements include President's Council from 1994 through 2006, Training Center Debut in 2005, being the first SEUL in her downline in 2007, being number one in Leadership in the Mid-Atlantic in 2012, and number 16 National in 2013.

When she is not working on her Avon business, Rosa enjoys reading. Her goal is to read at least six books per year. Rosa also spends time bird watching, taking pictures, and watching movies with her family on the weekends.

More A View From the Top
Volume 2

Now that you have been inspired by our stories and have learned a wide variety of tips, techniques and strategies to build a thriving direct selling or entrepreneurial business; the next step is to take action. Get started applying what you have learned in the pages of this book.

We want you to know that we are here to help you meet your professional and personal objectives. Below is a list of where we are geographically located.

You can find out more about each of us by reading our bios at the end of our chapters, or by visiting our websites listed on the next pages. When you call or email us, let us know you have read our book. We are here to serve you to enjoy your own view from the top!

Geographical Listings for *A View From the Top Volume 2*:
Avon's elite leaders share their stories
and strategies to succeed

Canada

Manitoba
Angela Kokorudz   www.interavon.ca/angela.kokorudz

United States

Arizona
Rosemarie Osolinsky   www.youravon.com/rosolinsky

Georgia
Pete and Gerry Colbath   www.youravon.com/gcolbath
DixieJean Cunningham   www.dixiejean.net

Illinois
Dan and Jackie Mundy   www.youravon.com/danmundy

Louisiana
Karen Tucker   www.karenbtucker.com

Maryland
Molly Stone-Bibb   www.youtube.com/molly7720

Mississippi
Tawana Lyles   www.youravon.com/tlyles

New Jersey

Marie Benoit-Wilcox   www.youravon.com/mbenoitwilcox

Esther Lunis   www.youravon.com/elunis

New York

Laura Douglas-Robinson   www.youravon.com/ldouglasrobinso

Claudette and Murtain Haskin   www.propeL92.com

Francine McDonald   www.youravon.com/fmcdonald

Ohio

Anita Albaghli   www.sellforsuccess.net

Lisa Scola   www.youravon.com/avonlisas

Jo Ann Potts   www.youravon.com/jpotts

South Carolina

Pam Heller   www.pamheller.com

Pam Knight   www.youravon.com/pknight

Chris and Gingermichele Kapp   www.youravon.com/gkapp

Texas

Kendall Cronk and Maria Delgado-Cronk

   www.facebook.com/avonsignsanddecals

Donna Reid-Mitchell   www.cydcyl.com

Maria Street   www.youravon.com/mstreet

Paula Weatherly   www.shopwithpaula.net

Virginia

Rosa De La O Gomez   www.youravon.com/rdelao

Carrie Purgason   www.consultantdepot.com

You're Invited...

. . .to join us for the **Business Breakthrough Summit** designed to give you tools to catapult your business growth.

The Business Breakthrough Summit is the right program for you if you want to create new streams of income, are ready to establish yourself as an expert in your field and are looking for a way of easily doing both. It is time for you to be one of the influential people in your field.

Join us at the Business Breakthrough Summit and in one weekend, you will gain the information and tools you need to accelerate your ability to easily add clients and learn how to be loud and proud about the value you bring to the marketplace.

Find out more about our next live event at: www.bizbreakthrough. com. Because you picked up and read this book, it is clear you have business savvy, therefore we have a gift for you. Enter coupon code BBSVIP50 for a 50% discount on your registration. Attend this event and watch your business thrive!

You're Invited...

. . .to join us for any of our Sought After Speaker Summits!

Do you have a message you want to share?
Are you ready to improve your speaking skills?
Have you seen how much influence people who speak have?
Would you like be a sought-after speaker?

In one weekend you can develop your public speaking skills and be loud and proud about the value you bring. Join us for our next live event at: www.soughtafterspeaker.com

Because you are savvy enough to pick up this book we have a gift for you. Enter coupon code SASVIP50 for a 50% discount on your registration. Attend this event and watch how your social status climbs!

Get Published With Thrive Publishing™

THRIVE Publishing™ develops books for experts who want to share their knowledge with more and more people. We provide our co-authors with a proven system, professional guidance, and support, thereby producing quality, multi-author how-to books that uplift and enhance the personal and professional lives of the people they serve.

We know that getting a book written and published is a huge undertaking. To make that process as easy as possible, we have an experienced team with the resources and know-how to put a quality, informative book in the hands of our co-authors quickly and affordably. Our co-authors are proud to be included in THRIVE Publishing™ books because these publications enhance their business missions, give them a professional outreach tool and enable them to communicate essential information to a wider audience.

You can find out more about our upcoming book projects at
www.thrivebooks.com.

Contact us to discuss how we can work together
on *your* book project.

Phone: **415-668-4535**
email: **info@thrivebooks.com**

Also from
THRIVE Publishing

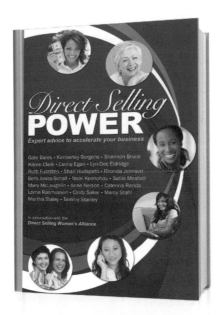

For more information on
Direct Selling Power, visit:
www.thrivebooks.com/store

Also from
THRIVE Publishing

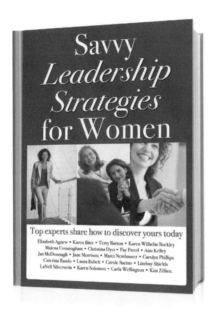

For more information on
Savvy Leadership Strategies for Women, visit:
www.thrivebooks.com/store

Also from
THRIVE Publishing

For more information on
Make Your Connections Count, visit:
www.thrivebooks.com/store

Also from
THRIVE Publishing

For more information on
Woman Entrepreneur Extraordinaire, visit:
www.thrivebooks.com/store

Also from
THRIVE Publishing

For more information on
Mom Entrepreneur Extraordinaire, visit:
www.thrivebooks.com/store

Also from
THRIVE Publishing

For more information on
Socially Smart & Savvy, visit:
www.thrivebooks.com/store

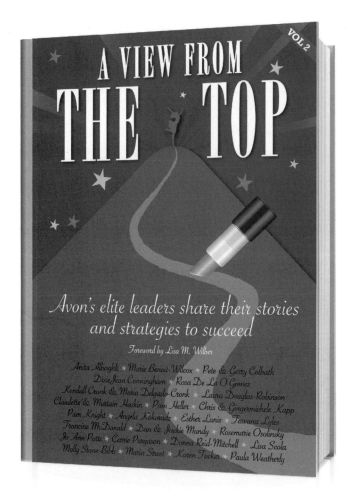

For more copies of this book,
A View From the Top Volume 2:
Avon's elite leaders share their stories
and strategies to succeed
contact any of the co-authors or visit
www.thrivebooks.com/store